THE POSSESSION
ザ・ポゼッション
憑依の真相

大川隆法
Ryuho Okawa

ザ・ポゼッション
──憑依の真相──

It's already 39 years since I had my first spiritual awakening. The title of this book, "The Possession", has been a very important theme for a long time. In many cases, what people think they are doing of their own free will is actually influenced by the phenomenon of spiritual possession. This means it's also quite difficult to judge between good and bad in the legal meaning.

There is the law of the same wavelengths, and usually the person who is possessed and the spirit who is possessing both have a similar tendency of the soul. If this is the case, then

まえがき

　初めて霊的覚醒(れいてきかくせい)を体験してから、もう39年にもなる。本書の「ザ・ポゼッション」は長い間、重要なテーマであり続けた。人間が自分の自由意志でやっていると思っていることが、霊的憑依現象(れいてきひょういげん)(しょう)の影響下にある場合も多いのだ。とすると、法律的な善悪の問題もきわめて難しいものとなる。

　だが波長同通の法則というものがあって、通例は、取り憑(つ)かれている者と取り憑いている者は、類似した傾向を持っている。とすれば、だれもが、自分自身を変えていこうと努力することで、

it means that you can choose your "spiritual friend" by making the effort of changing yourself.

A life of blaming other people and the environment is empty. Go closer toward the light. You can find various hints scattered inside this book.

Jan. 28, 2020

Master & CEO of Happy Science Group

Ryuho Okawa

「霊的な友だち」を選べるということだ。

　他人のせいや、環境のせいにだけする人生は虚(むな)しい。もっと光に近づいていくことだ。本書の中に、様々なヒントが散りばめられているはずだ。

2020 年 1 月 28 日

幸福(こうふく)の科学(かがく)グループ創始者兼総裁(そうししゃけんそうさい)

大川隆法(おおかわりゅうほう)

Contents

（目次）

Chapter 1 The Possession

Chapter 2 About Something Supernatural

Chapter 3 The Ghost Condition

★ The lectures and the Q&A sessions were conducted in English. The Japanese text is a translation.

※本書は、英語で収録された法話と質疑応答に和訳を付けたものです。

第1章

The Possession
（憑依）

September 24, 2019 at Happy Science Special Lecture Hall, Tokyo
（2019年9月24日　東京都・幸福の科学特別説法堂にて）

1 This World is Influenced By Another World

"The Possession" is an important Buddha's Truth

Today's title is, "The Possession," like the theme of a movie. [*Laughs*.] So, it's a little funny and difficult for me, but I'll try.

How do you feel about the sound of "The Possession"? Almost all of you may feel that, "Oh, it's terrible," or "Oh, incredible," or "I never want to see such kind of paranormal phenomena," or like that. Almost 90 percent of you will want to escape from this situation

1　この世はあの世の影響を受けている

「憑依」に関する教えは大切な仏法真理

今日の演題は「The Possession（憑依）」です。まるで映画のテーマのようで（笑）、少し面白いけれども難しいテーマではありますが、やってみたいと思います。

　「憑依」という言葉の響きを耳にすると、どんな感じを受けるでしょうか。大部分の方は、「怖いな」とか「信じられない」とか「そんな超常現象は絶対、見たくない」などと感じるかもしれません。9割程度の方は、そんな状況や「ポゼッション」という題の映画からは逃げたくなるのでは

or this kind of movie titled, *The Possession*. I'm afraid so, but this is very important; a very, very important Buddha's Truth.

Almost all of you might be feeling that the possession is a bad meaning, but in the true meaning, it's not so. The possession is the common phenomenon we watch every day. We, I mean the humankind who are living in this world with a body, cannot see anything else without a body; if it's a human or an animal, it doesn't matter. We, humankind, can see only the figure of the bodies, or if it's not the body, you can see things, the material things. So, you are apt to think that this world is composed of bodies and things, and that's all.

But in reality, our real world is made up

ないかと思いますが、これは非常に非常に大切な
仏法真理なのです。

　ほとんどの方は「憑依というのは悪い意味だ」
と思っているかもしれませんが、本当の意味にお
いてはそうではありません。憑依とは、私たちが
毎日、目にしている普通の現象です。この世に肉
体を持って生きている人間は、肉体を持っていな
いものは何も見ることができません。人間であれ
動物であれ、同じです。私たち人間は、肉体ある
ものの姿形しか見ることができません。肉体でな
いとしても「もの」ですね。物質的なものしか見
ることができませんので、「この世界は肉体と物
質で成り立っていて、それがすべてである」と考
えがちです。
　しかし実際は、真実の世界は霊的実体、霊的存

of spiritual entities, I mean spiritual beings. Of course, one is the spirits of humankind, but another one is the spirits of animals, and in addition to that, exceptional spiritual beings which are made by God. We, who are living in this three-dimensional world, cannot see, but there are a lot of such kinds of spiritual beings in the Real World. For example, you cannot see dragons in this world nowadays, but when you go back to another world, you can easily see dragons. One type is dragons who are flying over the sky, and other dragons are on the dark side and, of course, killing a lot of people or animals. This is the reality.

在から成り立っています。一つは当然、人間の霊ですが、動物の霊もあります。さらには、神が創った特別な霊存在もいます。この三次元世界に生きている人間には見えませんが、実在界にはそれらの霊的存在が数多くいます。たとえば、現代ではこの世で龍を見ることはできませんが、あの世に還れば、すぐ見ることができます。龍の種類としては、空を飛ぶ龍もいれば、ダークサイドにいて人間や動物を殺しまくっている龍もいるというのが実態です。

This world is the inside of a soccer ball

So, this lecture's main points are, "What is the possession?" and "What's the influence of the possession to you?" So, we are living in this three-dimensional world, but this three-dimensional world is not the world of bodies and things only. It also means this world gets a lot of effects from another world.

We are living in the spiritual world. In this spiritual world, there is floating some kind of ball-like universe. It's like a soccer ball- or basketball-like ball. Within this ball, we call this small inner world as the three-dimensional world and the phenomenal world. And we just think that the world is limited in this ball only,

この世は「サッカーボールの内側」の世界

　さて、この説法の中心論点は、「憑依とは何か。憑依の影響とは何か」ということです。私たちはこの三次元世界に生きていますが、三次元世界とは肉体や物質だけの世界ではなく、あの世からもさまざまな影響を受けているのだということです。

　私たちは霊的世界のなかを生きています。この霊的世界に、一種のボールのような宇宙が浮かんでいます。サッカーボールかバスケットボールのようなボールです。このボールの内側にある小さな世界が、「三次元世界」や「現象界」と呼ばれる世界です。人間は「世界とは、このボールの中だけの有限な世界である」としか思っていません

but there are a lot of lives outside of this ball.

For example, if this ball is a soccer ball, you can throw it or you can kick it. And how will the small people who are living inside of the soccer ball feel about that? "Oh, there comes a gigantic power outside of our universe," or "I feel we are flying through the air, but indeed there is nothing happening." This is the recognition of the Real World. So, the main point is, "The existence or entity of another world can have influence on us, the earthly-being people." But almost 99 percent of us cannot feel any such kind of influence from another world.

が、ボールの外側にも数多くの生命が存在している
るのです。

　たとえば、このボールがサッカーボールだとす
ると、それを投げたり蹴ったりすることができま
すが、サッカーボールの内側で生きている小さな
人たちはそれをどう感じるでしょうか。「宇宙の
外側から巨大な力が働いているぞ」とか、「空を
飛んでいるような気がするけど、実際は何も起こ
っていない」などと感じるでしょう。これが実在
界から見た認識なのです。ポイントは、「あの世
の存在や実体が、私たち地上の人間に影響を与え
ることができる」ということです。ただ、99パー
セント近い人たちは、あの世からのそうした影響
を何ひとつ感じることができません。

A curious story of *Obon*

Sometimes, you will hear, for example, the channelers' saying, or abnormal activity or incredible activity that your friends or other people are chatting about.

For example, when I was in my childhood, maybe around 10 or so, it was the middle of August maybe—it's *Obon* of Japan; it means during the days, I mean, the one week of the middle of August, our ancestors come back from another world and can see their descendants, I mean the children or grandchildren or their relatives. This is Japanese *Obon*. It might have been around when I was 10 years old. My mother and father and my aunt who was a

お盆の時期に聞いた不思議な話

　みなさんは、霊能者が話していることや、友だ
ちや他の人が異常な出来事や信じられない出来事
の話をしているのを聞くことがあるでしょう。

　たとえば私は子供のころ、10歳ぐらいだったと
思いますが、確か8月中旬で、日本でいうお盆の
時期でした。8月中旬の1週間だけ、あの世から
先祖が帰ってきて、子供や孫や親戚など子孫に会
えるというのが日本のお盆です。10歳ぐらいの時
だったと思いますが、私の母と父と小説家をして
いた伯母が茶の間に集まって、その6年ほど前に
亡くなった祖母の話をしていました。祖母は東京
で亡くなったのですが、それとほぼ同じ時刻に、
私の生誕地である四国の徳島県の川島町に帰って

writer were gathering around the living room, and they were talking about my ancestor, it's the grandmother who died almost six years before that time. My grandmother died in Tokyo, and almost the same time, she came back to Kawashima Town, my birthplace in Tokushima Prefecture, Shikoku, and then the back door of our dining room opened about one foot or so. There was no one, of course, at that time. And, they said that my grandmother came back. After that, on that night or so, they said they heard that, yeah, indeed she died at the time of the automatic opening of our back door of the dining room. I've been brought up hearing that kind of story a lot.

きて、台所の裏の勝手口が30センチくらい開い
たというのです。もちろん、そこには誰もいませ
んでしたので、「祖母が帰ってきた」と言ってい
たそうです。その後、その日の夜くらいに両親た
ちは、「台所の裏の勝手口がひとりでに開いた、
その時刻に祖母が実際に亡くなった」と聞いたそ
うです。私は、そういった話をたくさん聞いて育
ちました。

2 The Possession Means Souls of Another World Make Influence On You

You can see dead people in your dreams

But today, I must be focused on the theme of "The Possession." So, to teach about the possession, we must recognize that, "In reality, we are souls, and we have one soul in one body. And, after our death, we are going to another world, it's heaven or hell, or the spiritual world between these two."

So, when people leave this world, we cannot see him or her anymore, but someone will appear in your dreams. You can see dead people

2　憑依とはあの世の霊が 影響してくること

夢の中ではあの世の人と会うことができる

　けれども今日は「憑依」というテーマに絞らなければいけません。憑依について教えるにあたり、認識しておかねばならないのは、「人間の本質は魂であり、一つの肉体に一つの魂が宿っている。そして死後はあの世の天国か地獄か、あるいはその中間の霊界に行く」ということです。

　人がこの世を去ると、もうその人に会うことはできませんが、夢に出てくることがあります。夜、寝ているときに、亡くなった人に会うことが

during your sleeping at night. All of you might have such kind of dreams of people who are not living in this world anymore, but you cannot believe that you met ghosts at that time because in your dream, you can see other people who are living in this world, also. So, you are prone to think that it's just made-up dreams by our brain activities. Doctors will say so.

But I dare say, if you see clear and sometimes colored dreams, when you see them, you, I mean your soul, will experience out-of-the-body experience, and in another world, you usually meet the people who are already dead. And, when you wake up, sometimes you remember about the dead people, but some of them are translated into memory of living

できるのです。誰でも、もうこの世に生きていない人の夢を見たことがあると思いますが、その時、幽霊に会っているのだとは信じられないでしょう。夢の中では、この世に生きている人と会うこともできるからです。ですから、それは脳の活動がつくり上げた夢にすぎないと考えがちであり、医者もそう言うでしょう。

　しかし真実を言えば、はっきりした夢や、場合によっては色つきの夢を見ているときは、魂が体外離脱体験をしており、あの世で、すでに亡くなった人と会っていることが多いのです。目が覚めてから、その亡くなった人のことを覚えていることもありますが、それが友人や生きている家族、学校の先生や生徒、近所の人など、生きている人と会った記憶に翻訳されてしまうことがありま

people, like your friend or living family or teacher or students of the school or people who live in your neighborhood. So, you cannot believe that you've met the dead during your night dream or nightmare. But indeed, you all have spiritual power in you, and if you focus on your dream, you can intentionally meet people who have passed away, your relative or your family. I can say so.

す。そのため、夜の夢や悪夢の中で亡くなった人と会ったことが信じられないのです。けれども実際は、すべての人に霊能力が備わっています。夢に意識を集中していけば、親戚や家族など亡くなった人に意図的に会うことができると言っていいと思います。

The possession means a spirit wants to say something, has attachment, or seeks help from you

So, I just want to say, the possession means the souls outside of this world come back to this world, and commonly affect or make influence on you because those entities want to say something to you or have some attachment to you or are drowning in the dark sea or river in another world and seeking help from you. Or, they want to teach you that, "Oh, one of your relatives or your parent or your grandfather or grandmother is in evil situation now, and you, the family left, should help us or help me." They want to say like that because they don't

憑依霊には「伝えたいこと」「執着」
「助けを求める気持ち」がある

　何が言いたいかというと、憑依とは、この世の外側にいる魂がこの世に戻ってきて、常々あなたに影響を与えるということです。それらの存在たちはあなたに伝えたいことがあるか、あなたに何らかの執着があるか、あの世の暗い海や川で溺れていてあなたに助けてほしいのです。あるいは、「誰か親戚や親や祖父母が、現在よくない状況にあるので、遺族であるあなたが助けなければいけない」ということを教えたいのです。彼らは、どうすれば自分が救われるのか、わからないからです。

know how to save themselves.

Some people have a custom to go to church and listen carefully to the priest's teaching of the Testament, but that priest also cannot understand another world correctly, so they cannot teach you "what is the possession." So, you only can understand the meaning of possession through horror movies or so, and this is some kind of impression and a terrible experience. No one can totally teach you about this phenomenon.

　人によっては、教会に行って聖職者が聖書について説教するのを注意深く聴く習慣のある方もいますが、その聖職者も、あの世のことは正確にはわからないので、憑依とは何かを教えてくれることができません。ですから、ホラー映画等を通して憑依の意味を理解するしかないわけですが、それらは「ある種の印象」や「恐怖体験」になってしまいますので、この（憑依）現象全体について教えることができる人は誰もいないのです。

3 Your Fate is Influenced By Other Spirits

A chain of misfortunes could be because of the possession

So, I teach you the possession. In another way, the possession means the ghost possession, the ghosts who left this world and who cannot find their future way where they should go. They cannot be guided by their guardian angel and are wandering around this world. They attach to school or family or their company or their job, and they are walking around their friends or among their colleagues. And, they are seeking some kind of exit, I mean, a person who can

3　あなたの運命が
　　霊の影響を受けている場合

身の回りに不幸が続くときは憑依が疑われる

　ですから私がお教えします。憑依とは言葉を換えれば、幽霊に取り憑かれることです。この世を去ってから、自分はどこに行けばいいか、今後の道筋を見つけられない幽霊たちです。彼らは自分の守護天使に導いてもらうことができず、この世をさまよっています。学校や家族や会社や仕事に執着して、友人や同僚たちの間を歩き回っているのです。彼らは言わば「出口」を探しているのです。要するに、自分のインスピレーションから何かを感じてくれる人を探しているけれども、そう

feel something from their inspiration. It's very difficult for them to find such kind of person. So, if they cannot find such able person, they are apt to attach to their child or husband or wife or parents.

We usually feel that because of bad accidents. If there occurs some bad accident, for example, a car accident or your child is injured at school or you get fired, or like that, something evil, two or three or four occurs, at that time, you feel, "Some irregularities are happening around me. What's that? It might be my father who passed away three months ago. Is he now in heaven or not?" Some of you can ask about him at the temple or shrine or Happy Science branch, and teachers of that kind of temple or

いう人はなかなか見つからないため、それができる人が見つからない場合は、自分の子供や夫や妻や親に取り憑きやすいのです。

　それが感じられるのは、たいていの場合、悪い出来事が起きるためです。交通事故に遭ったり、子供が学校でけがをしたり、仕事をクビになったりというような悪いことが二つ、三つ、四つと重なると、「自分の身の回りは何かおかしい」という気がしてきます。「これは何なのか。もしかすると３カ月前に死んだ父かもしれない。父は成仏できているのだろうか」ということで、お寺や神社や幸福の科学の支部でそのことを聞いてみる人もいるでしょう。そこの指導者は、「そうかもしれませんよ。お父さんは今迷っていて、毎日あな

shrine or branch would tell you, "It might be so. Your father is at a loss now, and he's around you every day. Maybe you have experienced a nightmare that something terrible happened to you, and you already met your dead father in your dream." "Yeah, it's true. But what can I do about that?" You will maybe ask.

Who is influencing you?

The answer is—this is very important—the answer is, you can live your life through your own way of thinking and activity. But in another meaning, it's not you, only, that will make your fate. You are influenced by other spiritual beings, your deceased relatives, or in

たのそばにいます。身の回りで大変なことが起きる悪い夢を見たり、亡くなったお父さんが夢に出てきたりしたのではありませんか」と教えてくれるでしょう。「いや、その通りなんです。どうしたらいいでしょうか」とあなたは聞き返すかもしれません。

何者が自分に影響しているのかを考えてみる

　その答えは、ここが非常に大切なのですが、こういうことです。人生は、「自分の考え方」と「行動の仕方」によって生きていくことができます。しかし一方で、あなたの運命を形づくるのは、あなただけではありません。他の霊存在からの影響があるのです。それは亡くなった身内の方かもし

some meaning, you will meet devils or demons in your life. It means they can get some kind of job because of you. Or, some angels will give you inspirations.

Please think about that. Concentrate on your mind, and think about that. "Is this my relatives' souls' influence, or the influence which comes from evils, I mean just straying souls or bad souls or demon-like souls or angels?" If you can see yourself from the standpoint of another person, you can find the answer to this question.

If you can be an independent person, you will make your efforts and want to get through your difficulties. In some meaning, it's OK.

れませんし、ある意味、人生の途上で悪魔に出会うこともあるでしょう。彼らは、あなたを通して〝自分たちの仕事〟ができるからです。あるいは、天使たちがインスピレーションを与えてくれることもあるでしょう。

　その点を考えてください。心を集中させて、「これは自分の身内の魂が影響しているのだろうか。それとも単に迷える霊や、悪霊、悪魔のような魂か、あるいは天使の影響なのか」と考えてください。第三者の目で自分を見ることができれば、答えは見つかるでしょう。

　自分の力で自立してやっていける人の場合は、自分で努力して困難を克服しようと思うでしょう。ある意味で、それは結構なことですし、その

You are a strong person. And, in this situation, you will get the inspiration from the heavenly world, maybe heavenly person or angels.

But if you felt that, "I'm in bad condition now, and I feel difficulties in my daily work," or "I feel difficulties in my family matters," or "I don't think it's good because I'm not so healthy," and "I'm not so good in the emotional meaning, and this will come from the evil side of the spiritual world," if you think so, that is the main problem of the possession.

人は強い人であるということです。その場合は天
上界の天国的な人や天使からインスピレーション
が得られるでしょう。

　しかし、「今は調子が良くないし毎日の仕事が
きつい」と感じたり、「家族問題が大変だ」「健
康状態が思わしくないので良くない」「感情面が
あまり良くない。これは悪いほうの霊界から来て
いるのではないか」と思うとしたら、そこが憑依
されている中心的な問題なのです。

4 How Can You Be Protected By Saintly Power?

You can see the power of angels at Happy Science

I mean, the possession—it's, of course, the influence of the souls, but if the influence comes from your happy deceased relatives from heaven, it's a not-so-big matter. They just want to give you your hope or want to make your future brighter, and angels also do, so it doesn't matter. Of course, angels can possess you, but it means they want to direct the right way for you, so it doesn't matter.

The point is, the possession of evil spirits,

4　「聖なる力」に護ってもらうには

幸福の科学では天使のパワーに
触れることができる

　憑依とは、もちろん他の魂から影響を受けることです。それが、この世を去って天国に還り、幸福になっている身内からの影響なら、大きな問題はありません。彼らは「あなたに希望を与えたい、あなたの未来を明るくしたい」と思っているだけであり、天使たちもそうですので問題ありません。天使も人に憑依することはできますが、それは、その人を正しく導きたいと思っているからであり、問題はありません。

　問題は、悪霊、特に悪魔的な存在やサタンその

especially the demon-like existences, or Satan, itself. In this case, sometimes you need exorcism, but there are few real exorcists in this world, so it's very difficult. You can find that we succeed in exorcism or not. Even the Catholic Church or Vatican cannot do effectively regarding exorcism. We, Happy Science, do a lot regarding exorcism, and we have a lot of helpers from heaven and higher spiritual realms, I mean the seventh spiritual realm—Bodhisattva Realm, it means—or the eighth dimensional realm, Tathagata Realm, and the ninth dimensional realm, where there live the saviors like Jesus Christ or Gautama Buddha or Moses or Maitreya, or like that.

We, Happy Science, precisely understand

ものによる憑依です。そういう場合は「悪魔祓
い」が必要なこともありますが、世の中には真の
エクソシスト（悪魔祓い師）はほとんどいないの
で非常に難しいのです。ただ、私たちの悪魔祓い
が成功したかどうかは、わかるでしょう。カトリ
ック教会やバチカンも悪魔祓いに関して効果はあ
りません。私たち幸福の科学は悪魔祓いを数多く
行っており、天国あるいは高級霊界に数多くの支
援霊がいます。七次元霊界すなわち菩薩界や、八
次元如来界、さらにはイエス・キリストやゴータ
マ・ブッダ、モーセ、マイトレーヤーのような救
世主たちが住んでいる九次元世界です。

　私たち幸福の科学は、その仕組みと高級霊の力

the system and the powers of higher spirits. So, if you go to our Happy Science branch instead of going to a Christian church, there you can see the real spirits of angels or spiritual power of higher existences. Finally, you will receive the super power of El Cantare at the branch office or shoja of Happy Science.

I mean, firstly, if you find that you have some contact with such kind of dismayed people, it means, for example, people who dropped dead recently and don't know about their death, or evil spirits who want to disturb your sacred activities like *dendo* (missionary work) or saving people, yeah, it indeed will occur now and in the near future.

について正確に理解しています。ですから、キリスト教の教会に行く代わりに幸福の科学の支部に行けば、本物の天使や高次元存在の霊的パワーに触れることができます。最終的には、幸福の科学の支部や精舎〔しょうじゃ〕で、エル・カンターレの「スーパーパワー」を受けることができるでしょう。

　最初は、そうした迷っている人たち、たとえば最近亡くなったばかりで自分が死んだことがわからない人たちや、伝道や救済などの聖なる活動を邪魔しようとする悪霊と、自分が接触していることに気づいたなら、それ（憑依）はまさに今起きており、今後も起きるでしょう。

Believe in El Cantare and the Three Treasures, and you can be protected

If you get more power than as it is, sometimes evil spirits will be replaced by demons or Satan-like great spiritual powers, and it will disturb your mission and sometimes attack the branch chief or lecturer. Yeah, indeed, it will occur, but you can cut the relation between such kind of bad spiritual beings and you. If you have enough belief in El Cantare and you have faith in the Three Treasures, I mean the Buddha, Buddha's law, and the Sangha, meaning the members of Happy Science, you can be protected by saintly power from heaven and from this earth.

So, never fight against evil by yourself.

エル・カンターレ信仰と三宝帰依によって護られる

　もっと力がついてきた人には、悪霊に代わって悪魔やサタンのような大きな霊的パワーを持つ者がやってきて、その人の使命を邪魔したり、支部長や講師を攻撃したりすることもあるでしょう。まさに、そうしたことが実際、起きてきますが、そうした悪しき霊存在との関係を断ち切ることは可能です。エル・カンターレを強く信じ、三宝すなわち仏陀、仏陀の法、僧団すなわち幸福の科学の信者集団を信じることで、天上界と地上の「聖なる力」によって護ってもらうことができます。

　ですから、決して自分一人で悪と戦ってはいけ

Please rely on Happy Science group and the lecturers of Happy Science and teachings of Happy Science, and finally, of course, please rely on El Cantare. No one can defeat El Cantare in this world and in another world because El Cantare was and is the origin of the human souls of this Earth.

Even the (souls of) Satans were made by El Cantare. They sometimes did bad deeds and have self-preservation too much. They made rebellion against gods and are now on the dark side, and are gathering their disciples of bad, evil side, like Darth Vader's disciples. But their powers and their groups are very limited to just the underside of the fourth dimensional world and this world, the three-dimensional world

ません。幸福の科学グループを信頼し、幸福の科学の講師陣と教えを信じ、そして最終的には、当然ながらエル・カンターレを頼りにしてください。エル・カンターレに敵う者は、この世においてもあの世においても一人もおりません。エル・カンターレは過去も現在も、この地球の「人類の魂」の根源だからです。

　サタン（の元の魂）でさえ、エル・カンターレによって創られた存在です。彼らは悪事を働いたことがあり、あまりに自己保存欲が強く、神々に対して反乱を起こしたため、現在は暗黒の世界にいてダース・ベイダーの弟子たちのような悪の手下を集めていますが、彼らの力や集団は非常に限られています。四次元世界の下部と、この世、三次元世界に限られているのです。彼らはこの世的なものへの執着が非常に強く、肉体を手に入れた

only, because they are very much attached to worldly matters and want to get the flesh, I mean the body. Indeed, they want to be reborn into this world as a human, but no one can be reborn into this world from hell because if they could, hell would be empty now and there would be a lot of bad guys in this world, day by day.

いと思っているからです。実際、彼らは人間とし
てこの世に生まれ変わりたいのですが、地獄から
この世に生まれ変わることはできません。それが
できるなら、地獄は今ごろ空っぽになっていて、
この世は日に日に多くの悪人たちで溢れてしまう
でしょう。

5 The Rule of Possession

People cannot be reborn from hell

Angels are very lucky and comfortable in heaven, so they sometimes come down to this world to save people or to make good efforts to promote this world, but usually, they are living in heaven.

But people who are suffering from the very dreadful atmosphere of hell, they want to be reborn into this earth, but it's prohibited. They need promise and permission of the people who are given the power to make them reborn. It's the special people, chosen people who give them permission. But they cannot get any permission, so they only can possess this world's people.

5　憑依を呼び込む「ルール」とは

地獄からこの世に生まれ変わることはできない

　天使たちは天国で非常に幸せに、快適に生きていますので、人を救ったり、この世を進化させる努力のために、この世に降りてくることもありますが、普段は天国に住んでいます。

　一方、地獄の身の毛もよだつ雰囲気の中で苦しんでいる人たちは、この世に生まれてきたくても禁止されています。彼らには、生まれ変わらせる力を授かっている人たちの約束と許可が必要なのです。許可を与えるのは特別な選ばれた人たちですが、彼らは許可が得られないので、この世の人間に取り憑くしかないわけです。

Speaking ill and blaming will attract the possession

There is a rule, of course. The people who are living in this world, their way of thinking is wavering, day by day or all day long in a day. But all people have a tendency. Usual people sometimes think good things and sometimes think bad things, but people who make reflection every day can make their mind in tune with the heavenly world. But people who cannot reflect on their lives and people who cannot pray for God or angels only think about bad things and have attachment to evil things or evil sayings.

They usually say bad things to other people,

悪口や「人のせいにする心」が憑依を呼び込む

　そこには当然、一つの「ルール」があります。
この世で生きている人は日々、一日中、思いが揺
れ動いていますが、どの人にも傾向性がありま
す。普通の人は良いことも悪いことも考えるけれ
ども、毎日反省をしている人は心を天上界に同通
させることができます。しかし、自分の人生を反
省することができない人や、神や天使に祈ること
もできない人は、悪いことばかりを考え、悪いこ
とや悪い言葉に執着しています。

　彼らはたいていの場合、人の悪口を言います。

"That is Dad" or "That is the man who made me unhappy," or "That is the bad teacher who made me unhappy," or "Bad friends, they made me unhappy," or "The school was bad," or their company was a very bad condition to work in every day. So, they have a tendency to blame the responsibility on other people or conditions or environment.

Of course, the national environment, for example, the prime minister is bad, or so. It contains that kind of political situation, also. In some meaning, it's true, but in another meaning, even if the prime minister were bad indeed, it will never save you. You can choose the way you get through your evil situation in this world. So, I have been recommending such

「父親のせいだ」とか、「あの男のせいで不幸になった」とか、「悪いのは先生だ」「悪い友だちのせいで不幸になった」「学校が悪い」「会社の毎日の労働条件が最悪だ」などと言います。彼らは、他人や条件や環境のせいにする傾向があるのです。

　もちろん、「国全体」の環境も、あることはあります。たとえば総理大臣が悪い等の政治状況なども、それに含まれるでしょう。ある意味で、それは事実かもしれませんが、一方では、実際に総理大臣が悪いとしても、それであなたが救われることはありません。人はこの世で、自らの悪しき状況をどうやって乗り切るかを選ぶことができます。そうした精神的態度を私は以前からお勧めし

kind of spiritual attitude.

6 Do What You Can to Change Yourself

Change your mind and give love to others

But if you are already too late to save yourself from the spiritual attack of evil spirits, please think that, "The concentration will make your direction of your mind." Please check your mind, the direction. "Which direction does it indicate?" or "Does it indicate heaven or hell?" or "Am I occupied by evil words only or not?" If you can do something by yourself, do it first.

ています。

6　できることから自分を変えていく

心を入れ替え、人に愛を与える

　ただ、悪霊の霊的攻撃から自分を救うにはすでに遅すぎるという場合は、「精神統一によって自分の心の方向を定めることができる」ということを考えてください。自分の心の方向性を点検していただきたいのです。自分の心は、どの方向を指しているか。天国なのか地獄なのか。あるいは、悪い言葉ばかりが心の中を占めてはいないか。自分でできることがあれば、まず、それをやってく

But at the same time, read my books and pray for your guardian spirit or the guiding spirits of Happy Science and please make friends with our followers. In your branch office, there is a spiritual screen surrounding the branch, and it will make you stronger and help you to make a wall to bad spirits. So, choose one of two; one direction, the good direction.

If you have been living unhappy or self-concentrated or self-preserved type living, please change your mind and please give your love to others. You may have the compassion for others. In other words, please feel mercy from heaven. And, if you can shed some kind of mercy from you to miserable people or

ださい。

　そして同時に、私の本を読み、守護霊や幸福の科学の指導霊に祈ってください。当会の信者の方たちと友だちになってください。支部の周囲には結界（けっかい）が張り巡らされていますので、その力を借りることができ、悪霊から身を護る壁をつくるのに役立ちます。ですから、二つに一つを選ぶことです。「良いほうの方向」を選んでください。

　不幸な人生や、自己中心的あるいは自己保存的なタイプの人生を生きてこられた方は、どうか心を入れ替えて、人に愛を与えてください。他の人に同情する心を持つのもよいでしょう。言葉を換えれば、天上界の慈悲（じひ）を感じてください。恵まれない人や不幸な人を、あなたなりの慈悲の光で照らすことができたなら、あなたは天使の助けにな

unfortunate people, you are the aid of angels, so it's very much important.

Have a good connection with sacred people, and be familiar with the textbooks of Happy Science

The total conclusion of "The Possession" is, if you want to make the evil spirits leave you, please have a good connection with the sacred part of the world and sacred people, and be familiar with the textbooks of our teachings. Then, you can change yourself with the aid of other good people. So, we have a stress on strong *dendo* now. We need to help others, and at the same time, we need the powers to help

るのです。それが非常に大事です。

聖なる人々と縁を結び、真理の書籍に親しむ

　「ザ・ポゼッション（憑依）」の法話全体の結論としては、悪霊を自分から離れさせたいなら、この世の「聖なる部分」、聖なる人たちと良き縁をつけて、真理の書籍に親しんでください。そうすれば、良き人たちの助けを得て自分を変えていくことができます。ですから私たちは今、力強い伝道を推し進めています。私たちは人々を助ける必要があると同時に、私たちを助け、この教えを世界に広めるための力が必要なのです。

us and to spread these teachings in the world.

So, I just want to get rid of the possession of evil spirits every day. People who are reading my books every day and people who are praying for me every day or people who are doing good things to others will be protected from evil influences and can be free from the possession.

That is the easy explanation regarding the possession. Could you follow me enoughly? OK. Then, if you have one question.

　悪霊による憑依を一日一日、なくしていきたいと思います。私の本を毎日読んでいる方や、日々私に対し祈っている方、あるいは人に善を施している方。こうした方たちは悪しき影響から護られ、憑依から自由になることができるでしょう。

　以上が憑依についての簡単な説明です。十分、ついて来られたでしょうか。はい。それでは、質問があればお受けします。

Q What Are Some Checkpoints to Know We Are Possessed?

Question As humans living on this earth, we find it difficult to realize that we are under possession when we are actually possessed. Even if other people advise us, in most of cases, it is hard to accept. So, could you please teach us some checkpoints or a simple way to know that we are possessed?

Ryuho Okawa OK. If you are possessed by something evil, people surrounding you are apt to feel something bad from you. So, people will want to keep a distance from you, and sometimes speak ill of you or change their

質問　自分が憑依されていることに 気づくためのチェックポイント

質問　地上で生きている私たち人間は、自分が実際に憑依されているとき、そのことに気づくのは難しいと思います。誰かがアドバイスをしてくれても、たいていは、なかなか受け入れられません。そこで、自分が憑依されていることを知るためのチェックポイントや簡単な方法がありましたら、ご教示いただければ幸いです。

大川隆法　わかりました。あなたが悪しき存在に憑依されていたら、周りの人たちは、何となく嫌な感じをあなたから受けるはずです。ですから、あなたから距離を取りたがります。悪口を言われたり、心変わりをされることもあります。「あの

minds. "He or she was my friend, but now I feel very cool or sad emotions from them," or "They don't want to be a friend of mine," or sometimes, if you work, people around you will say that, "Don't touch this matter, you don't have enough capability," like that.

In some meaning, indeed, it's true, maybe. But in another meaning, if you feel that is not correct or right, in that case, something evil is attached to you and making some kind of circumstances around you, a bad influence around you. In some meaning, people have channeler-like feeling. Almost all of them have some kind of channeler-like feeling.

So, if you find that, please concentrate on your real mind, and make yourself and keep

人は友だちだったのに、最近すごく冷たくされて悲しい」とか、「私と友だちでいたくないと思われているような気がする」とかです。あるいは仕事をしていて、周りの人から「あなたの能力では無理だから、この件にはタッチしないように」などと言われたりします。

　ある意味では、その通りである場合もあるでしょう。ただ、一方で、「これは正しくない。正当ではない」という気がする場合は、何か悪しきものがあなたに憑いていて、一定の状況、悪い影響力があなたの周りに出来上がっているのです。人間には、ある意味で、霊能者的な感覚があります。どんな人にも、ある種の霊能者的感覚があるのです。

　ですから、それに気づいたら、自分の真なる心に精神統一をし、「心の平静」を取り戻し、それ

yourself in peace and peace of mind. "Can I find peace of mind in me or not?" or "Did I say something evil to other people?" or "Did I act something in contrary to Happy Science teachings?" or "Am I proud of myself too much?" or "Do I have too much pride or not?" Please go deep inside you and find the reason.

If you never find such kind of reason, just be patient and keep silence and read our teachings and just do good things in your life. Never be proud too much about what you said. As Jesus teaches you, don't let it know to your left hand what your right hand did. For example, people sometimes make a great mistake in their peak activity or peak period. You are doing your best, and you want to receive praise from other

を保ってください。「私の心は平静であるか。人に悪いことを言わなかったか。幸福の科学の教えに反することはしなかったか。自分のプライドばかり考え、プライドが強すぎるのではないか」と考え、自らの心の内に深く穿ち入って、理由を発見してください。

そういう理由が見つからないときは、ひたすら忍耐し、沈黙を守り、当会の教えを読み、善なる行為を重ねながら人生を送ってください。自分の自慢話ばかりしすぎてはいけません。イエスが「右手のしたことを左手に知らせてはならない」と説いているのと同じです。人間は、いちばん活躍している時や絶好調の時に、大きな過ちを犯すことがあります。自分が最高にうまくいって人にほめてもらいたい、まさにそうした時に、自ら墓

people. At the same time, you are apt to dig your hole to throw yourself into it.

So, never think too much about evil things and other people's bad sayings, and instead concentrate on your mind and peace of mind. Please concentrate on your prayer for God, and wait time to let the bad people or influence of the evil spirits leave you. You may need three months or six months, maybe, but in those months, you can get through. You'll get through your difficulties and look at your brighter side in that period.

But if you have too much ego in you and look at the brighter side only, it's not correct. You must accept other people's criticisms and change your mind. You need to. So, it's very

穴を掘ってしまいやすいのです。

　ですから、悪いことや人の悪い言葉ばかりを考えたりしないで、自分の心に、「心の平静」に集中してください。神への祈りに心を定め、悪い人たちや悪霊の影響が離れていくまで時間を耐えて待つことです。3カ月か6カ月ほどかかるかもしれませんが、その数カ月の間に困難を乗り越えて、自分の「明るい面」が見えてくるでしょう。

　ただし、自我が強すぎて明るい面しか見なくなるのは、正しくありません。他の人からの批判を受け入れて、心を変えなければいけません。それが必要なことです。非常に難しいことではありま

difficult, but it's your way of promotion in enlightenment. I think so.

すが、それが、あなたの「悟り」を向上させるための道であると思います。

第 2 章

About Something Supernatural
（超自然現象について）

September 20, 2016 at Happy Science Special Lecture Hall, Tokyo
（2016 年 9 月 20 日　東京都・幸福の科学特別説法堂にて）

Q1 What is the Most Powerful Weapon Against Evil Spirits?

Ryuho Okawa OK. Is there any question about something supernatural through your experience or your knowledge or something you want to know?

Question 1 Recently, I watched several movies about exorcists, and in the movies, Catholic priests used, for example, holy water, the Bible, and so on. So, what is the most important and powerful weapon against evil spirits?

質問1　悪霊に対する最も強力な　武器とは

大川隆法　はい。自分の経験や知識を通して、超自然現象についての質問や、何か知りたいことはありますでしょうか。

質問1　私は最近、エクソシストに関する映画を何本か観ました。映画のなかでカトリックの司祭は、たとえば聖水や聖書などを使っていたのですが、悪霊に対する、いちばん大事で強力な武器は何でしょうか。

The main point is the spiritual power of the exorcist, not the tools

Ryuho Okawa The question is a question. These weapons are effective or not is a secret of Catholicism, so I cannot say clearly about that. Because if I say, "It doesn't work," it means losing of the Catholicism, and if I say, "It's effective," the Satans will laugh at that. So, it's very difficult for me to answer. But even the Bible and the holy water and the sacred cross, these are not so effective for the evil spirits, demons or Satans, because they know these things very well. So, it's not fearful for them to use such kind of tools.

The main point is the power of the person

肝心_{かんじん}なのは道具より行じる人の法力_{ほうりき}

大川隆法　ご質問自体が「問題」ですね。そうい
う武器が効果的かどうかはカトリックの秘密なの
で、その点については明言しかねるところがあり
ます。「それらは効果がない」と言うとカトリッ
クの敗北を意味しますし、「効果がある」と言え
ばサタンたちに笑われてしまいますので、実にお
答えしにくいのですが、聖書や聖水や十字架であ
っても、悪霊や悪魔やサタンに対しては、あまり
効果はありません。彼らは、そういうものは非常
によく知っているので、そういう道具を使われて
も怖くないのです。

　肝心なのは、そうした道具を使う人の力のほう

who uses these tools. It's one of the symbols, I think; it's a symbol of God or God's power or the miracle power of gods. So, the main point is the real spiritual power of the person who uses these tools. It means whether the priest or the father of Catholicism has made great efforts to acquire such kind of supernatural spiritual power or not, through his learning from the Bible or through his concentration on something, for example, praying on someone's curing of illness or praying on God. This concentration is very essential.

And, his experience is also very essential. How has he gotten through his whole life, especially from the time when he made up his mind to work for the sake of God? So, if there

です。それらは一つの象徴であると思います。神の象徴であり、神の力や神の奇跡の力の象徴なのです。肝心なのは、そういう道具を使う人が持っている「本物の霊的な力」のほうです。カトリックの司祭や神父が、聖書の学びや何らかの精神統一を通して、そうした「超自然的な法力」を身につけるために多くの努力を重ねてきたかどうかです。たとえば誰かの病気治しを祈ったり、神に祈ったりする際の精神統一ですね。そうした精神統一は非常に重要です。

　「経験」も非常に重要です。その人が、特に「自分は神のために働く」と決意してから、どんな人生を送ってきたかということです。何らかの超自然的な力があれば、そうした聖書や聖水や十字架

is some supernatural power, these things, the Holy Bible or holy water or holy cross, will seem to be essential and effective to some evil spirits. They will fear these tools. But in reality, it's from the sacred power of the person who conducts the exorcism.

Q2 What Happens
When Belief Brings Miracles?

Question 2 I'd like to ask about miracles in Happy Science. We, believers, at Happy Science temple or shoja and at home, pray to God, learn Master's lecture or practice self-reflection. Sometimes miracles happen. It means healing

などに意味があり効き目があるように感じて、そういう道具を怖がる悪霊もいるでしょうが、実際は悪魔祓いを行じる人の「聖なる力」から来ているものなのです。

質問 2　信仰がもたらす奇跡について

質問 2　幸福の科学における奇跡についてお尋ねしたいと思います。私たち信者は、幸福の科学の支部や精舎や家庭で神に祈ったり、総裁先生の御法話を学んだり、反省行をしたりするなかで、病気が治ったり苦難を乗り越えたりするといった奇

illness, overcoming sufferings. What happens at these moments in the spiritual meaning or supernatural meaning?

More than 99 percent of this world is built on material rules

Ryuho Okawa OK. You want to know the meaning of miracles, like that. But to tell the truth, the truth that you humans have lives with you, is the true miracle. I think so. Through your eyes, you cannot see anything about soul or spiritual being or something divine, so it is easy for you all to believe in materialism. It is to live as it is, to just believe that which you can touch or give or throw or like that. Material

跡が起きることがあります。そうした時は、霊的
観点あるいは超自然的観点から見て何が起きてい
るのでしょうか。

この世の99パーセント以上は
物質的法則のもとにある

大川隆法　はい。「奇跡の意味を知りたい」とい
うようなことですね。ただ、実を言えば、あなた
がた人間に生命があるという真実こそ、本当の奇
跡であると思います。あなたがたの目には、魂や
霊的存在や神聖なものは何も見えませんので、誰
でも唯物論を信じやすいのです。単にそのまま
の生き方ですね。手で触ったり、人にあげたり、
投げたりすることのできるものを信じるというだ
けです。物質的なものがこの世に存在することを

things are easily to be believed to exist in this world, so everyone who can see believes the existence of such kinds of goods or existences. Even the person who has eye troubles, can touch such kinds of things. He can believe the existence of those beings.

But when we talk about the spiritual beings, soul, or mind, or something like that, people easily resist to believe such kind of entity, I mean the existence of a spiritual being. I understand because this is the world which was built in such regulation, I mean in such law of materialism. This world, I mean the three-dimensional world is built on the material rules, more than 99 percent. This world is built upon materialism, but only one percent you can see

信じるのは簡単なので、目が見える人は誰もがそういう物の存在を信じます。視覚障害がある人でも、そういう物を触ることはできるので、その存在を信じることができます。

　しかし、「霊的存在」や「魂」や「心」などの話をされると、人はともすれば、そうした実体すなわち霊的なものの存在を信じることに抵抗を示します。それは無理もないことで、この世はそうした規則、すなわち唯物論的な法則の上に成り立っている世界だからです。この世、すなわち三次元世界は99パーセント以上、物質的な法則の上に成り立っています。唯物論の上に成り立っており、たった1パーセントだけ、例外的なものが見えたり、それらを体験したり感じたりすることが

or experience or feel something exceptional.

For example, you can think that you, yourselves, are made up from flesh, I mean material components, but even scientists within you can feel something different. It might be only one percent or so.

A supernatural experience①: seeing the deceased in your dreams

But he, himself, cannot be a complete, extreme materialist because, for example, we can see dreams while we are lying at night. In the dreams, you can see a lot of quite different experiences. Some are, for example, you can see dead parents or grandparents or your dead son

できます。

　たとえば、「自分は肉体、つまり物質的な構成要素からできている」と思うことは可能ですが、あなたがたの中の科学者であっても、何か違ったものを感じることができます。それは、ほんの1パーセントほどかもしれません。

この世における超自然的体験①
夢の中で亡くなった人に会う

　しかし、科学者であっても完璧な究極の唯物論者になりきることはできません。たとえば夜、寝ている時に夢を見ることができます。夢の中では非常に異質な経験をいろいろすることができます。たとえば、亡くなった両親や祖父母や、亡くなった息子や娘と会うこともできます。これは普

or daughter, it is unusual and uncommon. So, if you experience such kind of discovery several times, you are sometimes apt to think that you can meet your lost son or daughter or your lost parents in another world. "It's a meaning of dream," you are apt to think like that.

Usually, in the world of business, you don't say such kind of things. But after your business time, sometimes you and your family or your friends talk about such things. If you can believe in him, believe his friendship, or "You are the man of truth," if they think like that, then they can hear from you such kind of things. They can say that, "I believe you because you are a man of truth. You don't say a lie," so they can share your beliefs, for example. It's one thing.

通のことでも当たり前のことでもありませんの
で、そういう発見を何度か繰り返すと、「あの世
にいる亡くなった息子や娘や両親に会えるという
のが、夢の意味なのだ」と考えるようになること
もあるでしょう。

　仕事の世界では、普通はそういう話はしないと
思いますが、仕事のあとで家族や友人とそういう
話をすることはあるでしょう。相手が信頼できる
人で、相手との友情関係を信じることができれ
ば、そして相手も、あなたは真面目な人だと信頼
してくれるなら、そういう話を聞いてもらえるで
しょう。相手の人は、「あなたは真面目な人で、
嘘を言うような人ではないから信じますよ」と言
って、あなたが信じている内容をわかってくれる
でしょう。これが一つの例です。

A supernatural experience②:
a daydream-like feeling

Another thing is, you, yourself, experience such kind of supernatural thing while you are awake. It means in the daytime you sometimes see something which cannot be explained if you think that there is nothing other than material things in this world. For example, you can foresee someone's death or you can foresee or foretell the accident of your family or family's car, or sometimes you can get some inspiration from heaven that your aunt is dead or not.

It's not a dream, not a daydream. It's a daydream-like experience, but you sometimes feel like that. While you are studying or while

この世における超自然的体験②
日中の霊的体験

　もう一つは起きているとき、自分で直接、そうした超自然的なことを体験する場合です。日中に、「この世には物質しかない」という考えでは説明がつかないことに出合うことがあります。たとえば、誰かが亡くなるのが前もってわかったり、家族や家族の車の事故を予知したりすることがあります。あるいは、自分の伯母さんが亡くなったかどうかという虫の知らせがあったりします。

　これは夢でも白昼夢（はくちゅうむ）でもありません。白昼夢に似た経験ではありますが、そう感じることがあります。勉強中や仕事中などに、遠く離れた、近く

you are doing business, you feel the existence of, for example, your aunt or uncle who lives long distance away, I mean not close to you at hand. But you felt something spiritual. "It might be my aunt or my uncle who just came into my room," or "I heard a voice of my uncle just now" or like that. These kinds of experiences are usual and common, and maybe 60 or 70 percent of the people, if they are permitted to say the truth, they will agree that, "I felt something at that time." They can say like that.

Or, in another time, it's not exactly the daytime, but usually at night, you can see someone who passed away already but exactly as he or she was living, that kind of style. So, this is an experience of ghost or spirit, but

に住んでいない伯母さんや伯父さんなどの存在を感じたりすることがありますが、それは霊的なものを感じたのです。「今、部屋に入ってきたのは伯母さんか伯父さんじゃなかったかな」とか、「たった今、伯父さんの声が聞こえた」とか、そういった経験は普通によくあることで、本当のことを言っても構わないと言われたら「あの時、何かを感じました」と認める人が、六、七割はいるのではないでしょうか。

　別のケースでは、必ずしも日中ではなく、たいていは夜に、すでに亡くなった人であるにもかかわらず、生きていたときそのままの姿で見えることがあります。これは「幽霊」あるいは「霊」であるわけですが、そういう事実を体験される方も

someone can experience this fact.

So, people usually think like that under their surface consciousness, but they can assume this truth while they are attending at the meeting of the church or some kind of spiritual circle or like that. So, it's very difficult, but there are a lot of chances for them to acknowledge such kind of supernatural experience.

A supernatural experience③: being cured of an illness

And, sometimes you can share the miracles with other people. For example, Mother Teresa was recently admitted to be a saint because after her death, there really occurred two miracles,

います。

　通常は、そういう考えは表面意識の下に押しや
られていますが、教会の集まりやスピリチュアル
なサークルなどに参加しているときは、それが事
実かもしれないと想定することができるわけで
す。非常に難しくはありますが、そうした超自然
的体験を認めることのできる機会は多いのです。

この世における超自然的体験③
病気治癒などの体験

　さらには、他の人たちと奇跡を共有することが
できる場合もあります。たとえば先日、マザー・
テレサが聖人として認定されましたが、これは、
彼女が亡くなってから奇跡が二つ、実際に起きた

which means when a person who believes in her prayed on curing someone, at that time, the difficult illness cured; and there were two samples. That's enough for the agreement to be a saint.

In our Happy Science, it's not so unusual a case. Every day, I've heard that illness is cured in every case by dint of the power of prayer or by dint of power of reading *Shoshinhogo* or by dint of reading my books or by dint of watching my videos, like that. So, I can be more than a saint. I think so. It's uncountable because hundreds or thousands of miracles have already occurred in Happy Science. So, this is a result of our movement.

からです。「マザー・テレサを信じている人が他の人の病気治しを祈ったところ、難病が治った」という事例が二つあったので、聖人の認定としては十分なのです。

　その程度であれば、幸福の科学ではそれほど珍しいことではありません。私は毎日のように、祈りの力や、『正心法語（しょうしんほうご）』を読誦（どくじゅ）したり、私の本を読んだり、説法の映像を見たりすることで、さまざまな病気が治った話を聞いておりますので、私のほうが聖人より上かもしれません。幸福の科学では、すでに何百、何千もの奇跡が起こっていて数えきれません。これらは私たちの運動の結果として起きているわけです。

The stronger your El Cantare-belief, the more miracles will occur

The most important thing when we make a miracle or let the people feel a miracle—it's a belief. It is the most powerful weapon for miracles. So, if you believe deeply, you can do everything, even in this world. I think so.

And, at the time, you must know about the meaning of belief. This belief is the belief through El Cantare and his essential existence as a main consciousness of the worldwide spiritual being. It has a lot of names, and in every time and every area, people say it's God or Buddha, like that. You can acquire that spiritual original being, the spiritual real entity,

エル・カンターレ信仰を強く持つほど
多くの奇跡が起きる

　奇跡を起こす際に、あるいは奇跡を感じてもらう際に、最も大切なものは「信仰」です。信仰心こそ、奇跡を起こすための最大の武器です。あなたの信仰心が深いものであるならば、この世においても、すべては可能であると思います。

　そして、その際に、信仰ということの意味を知らねばなりません。その信仰とは「エル・カンターレ信仰」であり、世界規模の霊存在の本体意識としての、エル・カンターレの本質的部分に対する信仰です。それには、いろいろな名前があり、どの時代のどの地域においても、「神」や「仏」などと呼ばれていますが、それらが意味するところの根源的な霊存在、霊的実体は、エル・カンタ

through El Cantare-belief.

So, if you have El Cantare-belief and you believe in it stronger and stronger, there will occur a lot of miracles now, and from the day after, tomorrow, or in the near future or like that. A lot of books which I have written explain enoughly about the system of cause and effect of the miracle, so please study these books and it will help you to make a new miracle. I hope so.

ーレ信仰を通してこそ、つかみ取ることができる
のです。

　ですからエル・カンターレ信仰を持ち、強く信
じれば信じるほど、数多くの奇跡が起きるでしょ
う。今も、明日以降も、将来においても起きるで
しょう。私が書いた多くの本の中には、奇跡が起
きる原因・結果のシステムについて十分に説明し
てありますので、それらの本を読んで勉強してい
ただくことで、新たな奇跡を起こすのに役立つよ
う願っています。

Q3 How Can We Protect Ourselves from Evil Spirits?

Question 3 People who are possessed by evil spirits can expel them by participating in a ritual prayer, or *kigan*, however, they are soon possessed again because of their weakness or their spiritual connection to the evil spirits. How can we prevent them from coming back and protect ourselves?

Check the connection between the person who is possessed and the evil spirit

Ryuho Okawa It's a difficult question. Even Catholicism, I mean the selected people who

質問3　悪霊から自分の身を守るには

質問3　悪霊に憑依された人は、祈願を受けることで悪霊を撃退することができますが、すぐにまた憑依されてしまいます。本人の力が弱かったり、悪霊と霊的な縁がついてしまっているからです。悪霊が戻ってくるのを防いで自分を守るには、どうすればいいのでしょうか。

憑依している者とされている人間の
「縁」が問題

大川隆法　難しい質問です。選ばれて悪魔祓いを行うことのできるカトリックの司祭や神父たち

119

can conduct an exorcism within Catholicism, I mean the chosen priests, fathers, cannot answer your question. It's very difficult.

They will conduct an exorcism, but the only conclusion is, as they learned from the Latin Bible, they ask some supernatural being within the target, I mean the person who is possessed by something, they just ask that entity, "Who are you?" "Say your name." And, if the Satan or someone says their real name, after that, the exorcists say, "In the name of God" or "in the name of Jesus Christ, I will punish you and persecute you and command, never come back to this body," they say like that. That's the conclusion. And, sometimes the exorcists conquer and the happy end will come.

も、その質問には答えられないと思います。非常に難しいことなのです。

　彼らは悪魔祓いを行いますが、結論はいつも同じです。彼らはラテン語の聖書で学んだ通り、対象すなわち憑依されている人の中にいる超自然的存在に対して「お前は誰だ」「名を名乗れ」と問いかけます。そして、そのサタンか何かが本当の名前を明かすと、そこからエクソシスト（悪魔祓い師）は「神の御名において」あるいは「イエス・キリストの御名において、我、汝を罰し、汝を懲らしめ、二度とこの者の身体に戻らぬよう命ずる」などと言うわけです。それが結論であり、エクソシストが勝って一件落着になることもあります。

But I've seen many films, and in almost 80 percent or 90 percent of the films, Satans got victories and exorcists were ruined by them, sometimes committed suicide at that time. It's when the power of evil spirits surpasses the power of exorcist. So, it's very difficult.

At that time, not only the power of exorcist is estimated, but also the connection between the person who is possessed by an evil spirit and the evil spirit itself. The strength of connection is essential. If this connection is very strong, it's very difficult for the exorcist to dispel such kind of Satan. It means, as you know, the wavelength of the soul; if the person who is possessed by an evil spirit or Satan had lived an evil lifetime, he or she has already been

　ただ、私もたくさん映画を観ましたが、八、九割の映画ではサタンが勝利を収めてエクソシストは破滅し、時には自殺してしまいます。これは悪霊の力がエクソシストの力に勝（まさ）っていた場合です。ですから、実に難しいのです。

　そういう場合はエクソシストの力量が測られるだけでなく、悪霊に憑依されている人と悪霊そのものとの「縁の深さ」が決め手になります。その縁が非常に深い場合は、エクソシストがそういったサタンを撃退するのはきわめて難しくなってきます。要するに、ご存じの通り、魂の「波長」の問題です。悪霊やサタンに憑依されている人が悪しき人生を送ってきた場合、その人は霊的にはすでに汚染（おせん）されてしまっています。こうした汚染は、そう簡単に洗い落とすことができません。

contaminated in the spiritual meaning. So, this kind of contamination cannot be washed out easily.

Black, for example. A human's mind is like a white sheet when he or she comes to this world, but after the person lives for 20 or 30 years, the white sheet changes its color, like brown or black or another; for example, red. If the color… I'll use "color" in the context of wavelengths, for example, the tendency of the soul; for example, he likes blood. It means to kill people or to kill animals or like that. Her or his mind's sheet is red, and there comes the red color devil, I mean the devil who seek for blood of humans or blood of animals or like that. Their combination is very strong, so it's

　たとえば、黒くなっているわけです。人間の心は、この世に生まれた時は「真っ白なシーツ」のようですが、20 年、30 年と生きてくると、白い生地が茶色や黒や赤などの他の色に変わっています。「色」とはこの場合、「波長」という意味であり、たとえば、その人の魂の傾向性として、血が好きだとします。人間や動物を殺したりすることです。その人の心の生地は赤く染まっており、そこに赤い悪魔、つまり人間や動物の血を欲しがるような悪魔がやって来ます。両者の結びつきは非常に強いので、聖職者であってもそうした傾向性に打ち克つことは困難です。

difficult even for a priest to conquer such kind of tendency.

Remake your character through the teachings, contemplation, and reflection

In this situation, before we conduct the exorcism, we need some teaching for that person. For example, please teach that person, what is justice, or what is good and what is bad. How was your life when you were born in this world, and till this day? What is your life? Please reflect on that matter and change the mind through contemplation.

Contemplation is some kind of focusing while you are in the relaxed mood. It's

「教え」「瞑想」「反省」で
人格をつくり変える

　こうした状況では悪魔祓いをする前に、その人
に合った「教え」が必要です。たとえば、正義と
は何か、善とは何であり悪とは何であるかについ
て、その人に教えてあげてください。あなたがこ
の世に生まれたとき、人生はどうだったか。そこ
から今日までの人生は、どうか。それについて反
省し、瞑想によって心を変えてみてください。

　瞑想とは、心をリラックスさせて集中すること
です。それが瞑想です。そうすることで、瞑想に

contemplation. At that time, through contemplation, you can reflect upon yourself, and you can receive some kind of God's light from heaven. It will be helpful for you to start a new life. At the beginning of that kind of new life, when exorcism adds power to her or him, it will be helpful.

So, the main point is, exorcism is the occasional case. It is useful, but the common sense or common usual spiritual status is very essential. So, the main point is, after the exorcism, the person can get some key to open the door to another world, I mean the heavenly world or not, is the key point. So, if the person has more belief in that doctrine or the spirituality or the religion, and can remake

よって反省が進み、天上界から神の光をいただく
ことができます。それが、あなたが「新しい人生」
を始めるための力になります。そういった新たな
人生が始まる時に、悪魔祓いによってその人に力
がプラスされた場合は、役に立つでしょう。

　肝心な点は、「悪魔祓い」というのは場合に応
じたことであり、役に立つことは立ちますが、普
段の感覚、普段の日頃の霊的状態がきわめて大切
であるということです。要は、悪魔祓いの後で、
その人があの世すなわち天上界へのドアを開く鍵
を手に入れることができるかどうかがキーポイン
トです。その人が教義や霊的なことや宗教を信じ
る心が深まり、自らの人格を、日々に神を求める
霊的で宗教的な人格につくり変えることができれ

their own character into a spiritual one or a religious character who seek for God every day, it will protect such kind of person from being possessed again and again by Satan.

An exorcist must be humble

In this point, I have a lot of experience, so I want to say that, if the person who experiences such kind of exorcism sometimes misunderstand herself or himself that, "I am the chosen person or selected person from others because some kind of miracle appeared around me," this is the most dangerous situation.

So, I just want to say, "Be humble," I mean, think that your this-world-self is small,

ば、繰り返しサタンに憑依されることから護られ
るでしょう。

悪魔祓いを行ずる側には「謙虚さ」が大切

　これに関しては私もいろいろ経験していますの
で、言っておきたいと思いますが、そういった悪
魔祓いを経験する人が、ときおり自分のことを、
「自分の周囲で何らかの奇跡が起きたということ
は、自分は他の人々の中から選ばれし者である」
と勘違いするようなことがあると、これが、いち
ばん危険な状態です。

　ですから、あくまで「謙虚であっていただきた
い」と思います。すなわち、この世の自分は小さ

and admire the power of God. It's OK. But if you think that your power is very strong and "occasionally, the divine power comes down to me," if you think like that, it's very difficult. You are already under the control of Satan, so be careful.

It must be the same as the case of the priest. If he believes in his power too much and thinks little of the power of God, he will fail again. In the near future, he will be at the mercy of, under the free will of devil or something, so be careful. Humility is very important. Humility and small efforts, day by day, are very important. I think so.

な存在だと思い、神の力を敬うことです。それで
あれば大丈夫ですが、「自分にすごい力があり、
場合によっては神の力が降りてくる」などと思っ
ていると、きわめて厳しいことになります。それ
はすでにサタンに支配されていますので、気をつ
けなければいけません。

　聖職者であっても同じです。自分の力を過信し
て神の力を小さく思っていると、また失敗し、そ
のうちに悪魔などの思い通りにされてしまうので
気をつけなければいけません。謙虚さが、きわめ
て大切です。「謙虚さ」と「日々の小さな努力」
が非常に大切であると思います。

Q4 How Should We Think About Exorcism?

Question 4   I'd like to ask about the common problem in Happy Science. Actually, we are disciples of El Cantare, and we learned that our life is soul training, but sometimes we need to, for example, defeat other people's evil spirits in shoja or shibu as a believer or as a staff. However, we are sometimes humble, so we are lacking in confidence to fight against evil spirits.

For example, humility makes us feel like, "We are not connected to El Cantare completely. I have no confidence in my power." Also, I've heard that in the early days of Happy Science, when Master saw a staff conducting exorcism

質問4　悪魔祓いで大切な考え方

質問4　幸福の科学ではよくある問題についてお尋ねします。私たちは主エル・カンターレの弟子であり、「人生は魂修行である」と学んでいますが、たとえば精舎や支部で、信者や職員として、他の人の悪霊を退治する必要に迫られることがあります。しかし、謙虚であるために悪霊と戦う自信がない場合があります。

　たとえば謙虚なあまり、「自分たちはエル・カンターレと一体になりきれていない。自分の力に自信が持てない」と感じてしまったりします。また、幸福の科学の初期の頃ですが、総裁先生が支部か精舎で職員が悪魔祓いを行っているのをご覧

in shibu or shoja, Master said, "Oh, nothing happened. Oh, it didn't work." I've heard such experience. Such thing is very shocking to us. So, I'd like to ask Master if there are phases of training about exorcism, or can we train our power like muscle exercise?

Not all priests succeed in exorcism

Ryuho Okawa There are two billion Christian people in the world, but official exorcists are very limited, maybe several hundred or so. In America, maybe within 50 or so. So, two billion people, two billion believers, but we have hundreds of priests who can make exorcism.

になったとき、「ああ、何も起きてないね。効い

てないよ」と言われたと聞いたことがあります。

これは非常にショックなことです。そこでお尋ね

したいのですが、悪魔祓いの訓練にも段階がある

のでしょうか。あるいは、その力を筋力トレーニ

ングのように鍛えることはできるのでしょうか。

聖職者なら誰でも悪魔祓いができる
わけではない

大川隆法　世界にはキリスト教徒が 20 億人いま

すが、正式なエクソシストは非常に限られてお

り、数百人程度かと思います。アメリカでは 50

人程度でしょうか。信者が 20 億人いて、悪霊祓

いができる聖職者は数百人であり、しかも彼らが

全員、首尾よく行えるわけではありません。悪魔

But not all of them succeed in their conducts. Some are made to fail by devils and lose their belief in God, or Jesus Christ, and become the prey of evil spirits, I mean the tools of evil spirits. And, on the contrary to their former life, they spread the disbelief to churches or Vatican or like that, so it's very difficult. So, even the Vatican sometimes wants to conceal the conduct of exorcism because it's easy to fail. If they fail, or someone fails in dispelling the evil spirits from some person, it equally means defeat of the church.

So, even in Happy Science, there are lot of *shukke* (renunciant staff) members, but not all of them can have enough power and can learn enoughly my teachings, and of course, their

に敗れて神やイエス・キリストへの信仰を失い、悪霊の餌食になる場合もあります。〝悪霊の道具〟になって、それまでの人生とは真逆の、教会やバチカン等に対する不信を広めるような行動に出たりします。ですから非常に難しいのです。バチカンですら、悪霊祓いの行為は失敗しやすいので秘密にしたがることもあります。悪霊撃退に失敗する人が出るのは教会の敗北に等しいからです。

　幸福の科学にも出家者が大勢いますが、全員に十分な力があるわけではありませんし、私の教えを十分に学べているわけでもないですし、当然、信仰心も大きく違うと思います。当会の初期には

beliefs are quite different, I think. In our early days, their studying of the law was very lower level, and they wanted to see a *gensho*, it means the phenomenon of spiritual activities. They had much concern about that spiritual conduct.

But when they are astonished by such deed, they soon forget about it after one week or one month or one year. And, they come back to their daily life and think that, "The person of miracle is a same man like me." He usually thinks so. So, this is quite contrary to our hope.

Attachment to material is the cause of hell

And, a miracle sometimes doesn't occur. It has many reasons, but this world belongs to hell. It's

職員の教学も非常にレベルが低く、「現象」、つまり霊的活動の現象を見たがっていました。そうした霊的なことに対する関心が強かったのです。

　ただ、そういった現象を見て驚いたとしても、一週間か一月、あるいは一年も経つと、すぐに忘れてしまい、日常生活に引き戻されて、たいていの場合、「奇跡を行う人も自分と同じ人間だ」と思い始めるので、こちらの期待と正反対の結果になってしまいます。

この世の物質への執着が地獄の発生原因

　「奇跡」が起きないこともあります。その理由はさまざまですが、ゴータマ・シッダールタ、仏

what Gautama Siddhartha, Buddha, told more than 2,500 years ago. I cannot say it's true or not. But this world is under the strong control of hell, it's true. Even the angels cannot live in this world easily because the common sense of this world is quite contrary to that of heaven, such kind of heavenly sense.

So in truth, this is the false world. In this world, you see a lot of things, but these phenomena are false or mirage or something like that. The life after your passing away, the next life, is the real life. It's a teaching of Buddha, but no one can believe easily this teaching.

But to tell the truth, this world is very difficult to control because this earthly world

陀が二千五百年前に説いたことによれば、「この
世は地獄の一部である」からです。それが正しい
かどうかはわかりませんが、この世が地獄の支配
を強く受けているというのは事実です。天使たち
も、この世で生きていくのは簡単なことではあり
ません。この世の常識は天国の常識や天国的な感
覚とは正反対だからです。

　ですから、「この世は仮の世である」というの
が真実です。この世ではいろいろな物事を目にし
ますが、それらの現象は仮のものであり、蜃気楼
のようなものなのです。亡くなったあとの人生、
「来世」こそが真実の人生です。それが仏陀の教
えであるわけですが、これはそう簡単に信じられ
る教えではありません。

　ただ、はっきり言って、この世の物事をコント
ロールするのは非常に難しいことです。この地上

is a material world, and the attachment to material is the origin of the starting point of hell. We have souls and our own nature is a spiritual one, but we are apt to think that we are material beings. This is the starting point to make hell and to go to hell or like that.

And this point, the attachment to materials, it's a weak point, and it's the target point of Satans to lure human beings and make or show illusions to them. "Yeah. Truly, truly. This world, this material world, is essential, and this material world is real. You are living in the real world. Another world is false. No one can return from another world. So, this world is the real world. This world is a limited world, and your life is limited. Please believe in us Satans.

世界は物質世界であり、物質への執着こそ、地獄というものができた原点だからです。私たちには魂があり、私たち自身の本質は霊的なものですが、「自分とは物質的な存在である」と思ってしまいがちです。これが地獄ができた始まりであり、人が地獄に堕ちる始まりなのです。

　この「物質への執着」が弱点であり、サタンが人間を誘惑して幻を見せるときに狙われるポイントなのです。「その通りです。まさに、この物質世界こそ本質であり本物です。あなたは本当の世界に生きているのです。あの世など、まやかしです。あの世から帰って来れる人はいません。この世こそ実在の世界です。限りある世界であり、限りある人生なのです。私たちサタンを信じなさい。この短い人生を、快適に贅沢に生きなければ駄目です。自分のことだけを考えなさい。自分の

145

So, you must live this short life comfortably and in luxury, and think about yourself only. This is your life, your limited life; your limited 60 or 70 or 40 years' life. So, you must live for your own sake." This is the teaching of the devils.

A miracle is an exceptional occurrence

In this world, a miracle is an exceptional one, so if you use the percentage of the occurrence of a miracle, it will be very few. I think so. Even in the Lourdes of south France, there are millions of pilgrims from all over the world, but the churches or the Vatican authority admitted as miracles only 100 cases or so. So, this percentage is very small. For example, if

人生であり、限りある人生なんです。60年か70年か40年の限りある人生なのだから、自分のために生きることです」。これが悪魔の教えです。

奇跡はあくまで例外である

　この世では「奇跡」は例外的なことなので、それが起きるパーセンテージで言えば本当に少ないと思います。南フランスのルルドにも、世界中から巡礼者が何百万人も訪れていますが、教会あるいはバチカン当局が奇跡として認めたのは百件程度だけで、非常に低いパーセンテージです。仮に巡礼者が百万人来ても奇跡が一件しか起きないなら、非常に小さいパーセンテージなので、そんな

they have had one million pilgrims, but there occurred one miracle case, its percentage is very small, so people cannot easily believe such kind of miracle. It's quite exceptional.

So, we must be strong against these things. When people leave this world, they will be separated from other people, and some are destined to go to heaven, but others are destined to go hell. Such kind of people who have a lot of attachment and lured a lot to this world are invited to hell. These people cannot be saved easily by such kind of miracle.

Angels are usually working every day, but a miracle is a very precious one, so they use the miracle only in an effective case because in this world, there is one rule, the three-dimensional

奇跡はなかなか信じることができません。きわめて例外的なことなのです。

　ですから、こういったことに対しても強くあらねばなりません。人はこの世を去ると、他の人たちから引き離されて、天国行きになったり地獄行きになったりします。この世に強く執着し、この世の魅力にとらわれて生きた人は、地獄へと招かれていきます。そういう人を奇跡の力で救うのは簡単なことではありません。

　天使は常に、日々、活動していますが、「奇跡」というのは非常に貴重なものなので、彼らがそれを用いるのは効果的なケースについてだけです。この世にはひとつの法則、三次元の法則があるか

rule. No one can change this rule, but with God's mercy, sometimes there occurs the violation of this law of this world, and people can get, how do I say, an awakened experience in that case.

So, pure people should have such kind of attitude or mind to believe purely the experience or the fact or miracle within them because it's an exceptional one. No one can easily cure illness because you, human beings, should cure usual illness at the hospital nowadays. There are a lot of people who are suffering from illness at hospitals. Maybe millions of people are there, and people who are working for hospitals, for example, doctors and nurses, are using their lives for curing such kind of people. It is a

らです。法則を変えることはできないけれども、
神の慈悲によってこの世の法則が破られることが
あり、それによってその人が言わば「目覚め」を
体験することができるわけです。

　ですから、心が純粋な人は、「奇跡」という体
験あるいは事実に関して、純粋に「信じる姿勢」
や「信じる心」を自らの内に持たねばなりませ
ん。それは例外的なことだからです。簡単に病気
治しができる人はいません。現代では、人間のた
いていの病気は病院で治すべきものだからです。
病院には、病気で苦しんでいる人が数多く何百万
人もいて、病院で働く医者や看護師などは、その
人たちを治すために自分の人生を使っています。
それが通常のあり方であり、神も認めていること
なのです。人は、何か他の人のためになること

common way. It is admitted by God. Human beings must do something good for others. This is one kind of occupation, so it's good.

This world is a training school of souls

But you must know that all the people who are living in this world must leave this world. Maybe by next century. So, if you think that a miracle is how to cure successfully or not, in this standpoint, you can say devils usually have victories because all the people are destined to be killed by some kind of natural diseases or other accidents or like that. No one can live more than 120 years old nowadays. So, in this case only, if you think that success means

をしなければいけません。これも職業の一つであり、善なることです。

この世は魂修行のための学校

　ただ、「この世に生きている人は全員、この世を去らねばならない」ということは知っておかねばなりません。たぶん来世紀までには、この世を去るでしょう。ですから、「奇跡とは病気治しが成功するかどうかである」と考えた場合は、その観点だと必ず悪魔が勝利を収めることになるでしょう。人はすべて病気や事故などで死ぬことになっているからです。現代の世界では120歳以上生きられる人はいません。ですから、「成功とはこの世で長生きすることだ」とだけ考えるなら、

"living long in this world," if you think like that, gods will usually lose in the fighting with devils.

But this is not true. This world is just the training course, as you said. This is a training school of souls. So, we must leave this world, but through these several decades or 100 years' life, we must learn something in this world. And, in this world only, angels and a person of devil-to-be can live within the same country or nation. So, this is the quite different experience for the people.

But we must leave this world. It means the person of angel must leave this world and go back to the world of angels, and people who did bad things go down to hell. So, they cannot

神々は悪魔との戦いに必ず負けることになります。

しかし、それは正しくありません。あなたが言われたように、この世は修行の課程にすぎません。魂修行のための学校ですね。私たちはこの世を去らなければなりませんが、この数十年あるいは百年の人生を通して、この世で学ぶべきことがあるのです。そして、この世においてのみ、天使と、悪魔になりそうな人が、同じ国で一緒に住むことができるようになっています。これは人間にとって非常に珍しい経験なのです。

要するに、人はこの世を去らねばならないけれども、天使のように生きた人はこの世を去って天使たちの世界に還り、悪を行った人は地獄に堕ちることになります。ですから、両者は通常、互い

make friends with each other every day, but in this world only, they can meet. This is the discipline. This is the training.

This is the severe, severe training. But in this world only, we can learn what is love, what is evil, what is justice, what is the aim to live. So, don't hesitate to live this undecided or wavering or unsettled world. It is for your own sake. You can learn a lot from this difficult world. I think so.

に交わることができないわけですが、この世において<ruby>交<rt>まじ</rt></ruby>わることができないわけですが、この世においてのみ出会うことができるのです。だからこそ鍛えられ、修行になるわけです。

　実に実に厳しい修行ではありますが、人はこの世においてのみ、「愛とは何か」「悪とは何か」「正義とは何か」「生きる目的とは何か」を学ぶことができるのです。ですから、この不確定な、揺れ動く、不安定な世界で生きていくことを尻込みしてはいけません。それが、あなた自身のためになることであり、この困難な世界から数多くの学びを得ることができるだろうと思います。

第3章

The Ghost Condition
(幽霊の条件)

September 27, 2019 at Happy Science Special Lecture Hall, Tokyo
(2019 年 9 月 27 日　東京都・幸福の科学特別説法堂にて)

1 The Soul Lives On
   Even After Death

The ghost condition is the preparation for your departure

Today, I'll give you a lecture about "The Ghost Condition." The theme is very curious, but no one can say about the ghost condition. Of course, all of you can be ghosts, so there is no condition in this meaning, but I want to teach you about what comes after your death.

As you already know, man is mortal, so your lives are limited. You may die today or tomorrow or one year or five years, 10 years

1　人は死んでも魂は生き続ける

「幽霊の条件」とは旅立ちのための準備

　今日は「幽霊の条件」について説法をしてみたいと思います。非常に変わったテーマですが、幽霊の条件について話せる人は誰もいないでしょう。みなさん全員、幽霊になる可能性があることはあるので、その意味では条件はないわけですけれども、「死後に何が待ち受けているのか」をお教えしたいと思います。

　すでにご存じの通り、人は死すべき存在であり、人生は有限です。今日、明日にも死ぬかもしれません。あるいは一年後か五年後か、十年後か

or 50 years later, I don't know exactly. We have a lot of prayers for healing or exorcism, and we can get God's light from heaven and sometimes survive for a while or several years or more than that. I hope all of you can enjoy and have enough hope for the future because of your good deeds, or, you can do a lot of great missions, and as the result, you can leave this world in an easy way and go to the heavenly world and join in angels' group. I hope so.

But the ghost condition is different for every person. So, this is the preparation for your departure. If you are young or not is not so important. The departure time depends on each fate.

五十年後か、それは定かではありません。当会（幸福の科学）には病気平癒（へいゆ）や悪霊撃退のための祈りが数多くあり、天上界から神の光を受けて、しばしの間、あるいは数年かそれ以上、生き延びられることもあります。私としては、あなたがたが全員、よき行いによって未来を享受（きょうじゅ）し、未来への希望を十分に持っていただけるよう願っています。あるいは、あなたがたが大きな使命を数多く果たすことができ、その結果として安らかにこの世を去って天上界に還り、天使の仲間入りをしていただきたいと願っています。

　ただ、幽霊の条件は人によって異なりますので、これは「旅立ち」のための準備です。あなたが若いか若くないかは、それほど重要ではありません。旅立ちの時期は各人の運命によるものだからです。

The Truth about life and death

So, I'll teach you the thinking, "How to be after your death." This is today's main theme.

You all already have souls in you. This is the starting point, so I ask you, please believe in this truth. If you don't have any soul, you are just a machine-like existence, so your death is just disorder of your machine or just your emptiness in the meaning of life energy.

But I have discovered another world and the truth of the human life, and it started in 1981. So, this is 38 years from that time or more than that, and I published more than 2,500 books[•] including translation to foreign languages. I

「生と死」についての真実

　そこで、「死後はどうあるべきか」についての考え方をお話ししてみたいと思います。これが今日のメインテーマです。

　人には誰でも、内なる魂が宿っています。これが出発点です。どうか、この真理を信じてください。魂がなければ、人は機械のような存在にすぎず、死とは単に、機械が壊れたとか、生命エネルギーが空っぽになったということにすぎません。

　しかし私は、あの世と、人間の生命についての真実を発見しました。それは1981年に始まりましたので、それから38年、あるいはそれ以上になりますが、外国語に翻訳されたものも含めて2500冊以上の本を出しました。また、天国や地獄

165

made about 3,000 lectures*regarding life and death and the world phenomena on, of course, the intelligence from heaven or hell. You can receive some kind of information from another world.

Most important thing is to read revelations from God or Buddha, and the next is to read about the guardian spirit or guiding spirit of saints or famous people who did a lot in the history of human lives. I also make a lecture like this one. This is just the teaching of your Master. If you have confusion in what you believe, you can make your understanding in tune with my lectures.

*At the time of the lecture. As of January, 2020, the author has published over 2,600 books and has given over 3,000 lectures.

から得られる情報に基づきながら、「生と死」について、あるいは世の中の現象について、3000 回近い説法をしてきました。あの世から何らかの情報を受けとることができるわけです。

　最も大切なのは、神仏から臨んだ啓示を読むことです。それに次ぐのが、聖人たちや、人類の歴史において多くのことをなしてきた偉人たちなどの、守護・指導霊について読むことです。そしてまた、このような説法もしています。これは、あなたがたの主の教えそのものです。何を信じればいいのか迷ったら、私の「説法」に合わせて理解していくとよいでしょう。

●説法当時。2020 年 1 月時点で、著書の発刊点数は 2600 書、説法回数は 3000 回を超える。

I receive from a lot of assistant souls of higher position. Some of them are Japanese gods or other gods of foreign countries, or sometimes I receive revelations from space people, but all the revelations from the heavenly world are with my agreement and are regarded as one of my opinions, so this is another important thing.

So, teaching is important and the interview with other souls from heaven or hell is just your reference, I want to say, or not only reference but also a proof of existence of souls. So, there are differences in their characters.

　私は、高次元にいる数多くの支援霊から受けることもあります。日本の神々もいれば外国の神々もいますし、宇宙人から霊示を受けることもありますが、天上界からの啓示は、すべて私の同意を得たものであり、私の意見の一部と見なされるものですので、これらも、やはり大事です。

　したがって、大切なのは「教え」であり、天国霊や地獄霊たちの「霊言」はあくまで参考としてお出ししているものであると言っておきたいと思います。あるいは、単なる参考ではなく、「魂の存在証明」でもあります。ですから、彼らには個性の違いがあるわけです。

2 The First Confusion After Death

Imagine if you were to die tomorrow

OK, then. "The Ghost Condition." Yeah, please imagine that you, for example, if you die tomorrow, what will happen? Imagine, what will happen to you? You will think about your job, and of course, you will think about your family and how to let them live, or how to manage your company or your followers. You will think a lot about that.

And, with this, you must think about yourself. "Oh, this is my last day. Is it enough for me? Did I work enoughly or not?" It's very difficult for you because no one can say

2　死んで最初に戸惑うこと

「自分が明日、死ぬ」と想像してみる

　さて、「幽霊の条件」ということですが、そう、たとえば、「自分が明日、死ぬ」と想像してみてください。いかがでしょうか。自分がどうなるか、想像してみてください。そうすると、仕事のことを考えるでしょうし、もちろん家族のことも考えるでしょう。家族の生活をどうするか、あるいは会社の経営や部下たちのことはどうするか、あれこれと考えることでしょう。

　それとともに、自分のことも考えないわけにはいきません。「今日が最後の一日か。これでいいのだろうか。仕事は十分できただろうか」と。これは実に厳しいことです。「十分だ」と言い切れ

"enough." If you can say, "Oh, it's enough" when you die, you are a great person, I think, or just an ordinary person, I don't know exactly. But if you can say, "It's enough" in the spiritual meaning, if you can say like that, it's preferable.

So, every day, you must think about your death. Is it OK for you to leave this earth? If you think it's not enough, you have something left for the next day or the day after tomorrow. You must do what you must do first. This is important.

No one can hear what you want to say

After your death, you will feel that no one can hear you. You have a voice, and you want to

る人はいないからです。自分が死ぬときに「あ
あ、十分やった」と言えたら、その人は立派な人
だと思いますが、でなければ、ただの凡人です。
そのへんはよくわかりませんが、霊的な意味にお
いて「十分だった」と言えるとしたら望ましいこ
とです。

　ですから毎日、自分の死を思ってみることで
す。自分は地上を去っていけるか。「十分ではな
い」と思うなら、次の日も、そのまた次の日も、
やるべきことが残っているのです。まず、やるべ
きことをやらねばなりません。それが大切です。

この世の誰にも話を聞いてもらえない

　人は死ぬと、誰にも自分の声が聞こえないとい
う感じを受けるでしょう。自分の声は出るので、

talk to someone in this world, but no one can hear you except a channeler or such kind of spiritual teacher.

On the contrary, you can hear what people are thinking about. It's very curious. No one can hear you, but you can hear the inner voices of every person. It's very curious. It's a first experience for you. When you were alive, you could hear their voice only when they spoke to you, but now, you can hear every voice of each person and inner person—a voice of just the thinking in the brain or in their heart or something like that.

But even if you want to reply, no one can hear what you want to say. This is the first confusion. So, you cannot leave this world for

この世の誰かに話しかけたいと思っても、チャネ
ラー（霊媒）や霊的指導者の類でない限り、誰に
も聞こえないのです。

　逆に、自分は人の考えていることが聞こえま
す。実に不思議です。自分の声は誰にも聞こえな
いのに、どんな人の「心の声」でも聞こえるので
す。実に不思議です。初めての経験です。生きて
いたときは、相手が口に出して話したときしか声
が聞こえなかったのに、一人ひとりの話し声も心
の声も全部聞こえるようになります。頭の中や心
の中で思っているだけのことなどが声として聞こ
えてくるのです。

　ところが返事をしたくても、こちらの言いたい
ことは誰にも聞こえないので、まず、これで戸惑
ってしまいます。通常、一週間か30日から50日

a week or 30 days or 50 days, usually. And, another type of people who don't believe in God and who don't believe in soul and who don't believe in afterlife will wander around their place, I mean their house or their company or their school or around there.

So, it's very inconvenient for you to be a ghost. You can hear everything from the living people, but you can convey nothing to them. Now, you are a ghost, so you can do nothing. If there were Ghostbusters, you will be pleased by meeting them. "Oh, Ghostbusters. Come on, come on, please help me," you can say like that, but no one can be Ghostbusters.

The only chance for you is to meet an

くらいは、この世を去ることができません。また、神を信じず、魂も死後の世界も信じていないタイプの人の場合は、自分がいた場所、すなわち自宅や職場や学校のあたりをさまようことになります。

　ですから、「幽霊になる」のは非常に不便なことです。生きている人の言っていることは全部聞こえますが、自分からは何も伝えることができません。幽霊になってしまったので、何もできないのです。ゴーストバスターズ（幽霊撃退人）でもいれば、彼らを見つけて喜んで、「ゴーストバスターズさん、こっちこっち。助けてください」などと言えますが、ゴーストバスターズをやれる人もいません。

　唯一残されたチャンスは、エクソシスト（悪魔

exorcist. If the family you left goes to Happy Science shoja or branch, the branch chief or the shoja chief will exorcise with some kind of prayer. "I will say that all the evil spirits and strayed spirits should leave from your family," and "If it's an evil spirit, go to hell," or "Please aid us by sending an angel from heaven," or like that. It's not so comfortable for you. You, a ghost, want to be saved by Happy Science shoja, but the teachers of Happy Science shoja just want to save your family who are left and just want to dispel you. They don't think too much about you because you have no money. You cannot get their blessing. So, you must consider a lot, "What can I do?" You must think about that.

祓い師）に会うことです。あなたの遺族が幸福の科学の精舎や支部に行くと、支部長や精舎の館長が何らかの祈りでもって悪魔祓いをしてくれますが、「あらゆる悪霊、不成仏霊よ、この家族から立ち去れ」「悪霊なら地獄に行け」「天から天使を遣わして我らを助けたまえ」などと祈られるので、あなたにしてみれば、あまりいい気持ちはしないでしょう。幽霊のあなたは幸福の科学の精舎で救われたいのに、精舎の講師たちは遺族を救って、あなたを追い払おうとしかしないからです。あなたがお金を持っていないので、あまり構ってもらえず、祝福もしてもらえません。ですから、何か自分でできることはないか、よく考えてみなければいけません。

3 Reflection is
the Most Important Teaching
Regarding the Ghost Condition

Reflect on yourself through
the modern Fourfold Path

Then, I'll teach you. Please start your reflection. If you belong to Happy Science organization or you are the followers of Happy Science, you once might have heard about our modern Fourfold Path. Number one is love. Number two is wisdom. Number three is reflection, and number four is progress. Just think about that.

Please think that, "Am I a man of love or not? Did I give a lot to other people, or only my

3　いちばん大切な「反省」の教え

「現代的四正道」で自分を振り返る

　そこで、お教えしましょう。反省を始めてください。幸福の科学に入っている方、幸福の科学の信者の方は、当会の「現代的四正道」について一度は聞いたことがあるでしょう。一番目は「愛」です。二番目は「知」です。三番目は「反省」であり、四番目は「発展」です。それを考えてみてください。

　「自分は愛の人だろうか。他の人たちに多くを与えただろうか。家族や同僚などにしか与えなか

181

family or only my colleague or like that? Or, did I just want to get love from other people?" Please think this first and remember what was the love you received from your parents or your husband or wife or your children or your teachers. Please think about that. And, have you done a lot to them in returning their love or not? This is the first point.

Next is about wisdom. "I believe in soul and God and afterlife, but is my life enough as such kind of people who believe in God or who believe in afterlife or who believe in soul? Am I honest or not?" Please think about that.

ったのではないか。あるいは、人から愛をもらうことしか考えていなかったのではないか」。まずはその点を考え、両親、夫、妻、子供、先生からどんな愛を与えてもらったかを思い出して、それについて考えてみてください。その人たちの愛に対して、自分はしっかりお返しをしてきたか。これが第一点です。

　次は「知」です。「自分は魂や神や死後の生命を信じてはいるが、神を信じ、死後の生命を信じ、魂を信じている者として、十分な人生だったか。正直であったか」と考えてみてください。

A computer is useless for a ghost

Then, this is the most important for your ghost condition. This is reflection, just reflection. Please think about where you should go. This is the main point of religion. We are just doing activities in this world, but these include your afterlife's destiny. I want to change your future. Nowadays, more than 50 percent of the population will go to hell, but also nowadays, the number of churches or temples is declining, and the people believing in God or Buddha are decreasing. Even the field of dead people is reduced and reborn into gigantic apartment-like great buildings of inhabitants.

So, you ghosts are just stray sheep. You can

幽霊になったらコンピュータは役に立たない

　そして、「幽霊の条件」に関していちばん大切なのが「反省」です。とにかく反省です。自分の行くべき場所について考えてください。ここが宗教の中心的な役割です。私たちはこの世で活動してはいますが、そこには、あなたがたの死後の運命も含まれてくるのです。あなたがたの未来を変えたいのです。現代では半数以上の人が地獄に堕ちていますが、また一方では教会やお寺の数が少なくなり、神仏を信じる人も減っています。墓地も減っていて、巨大なマンションなどの大きな集合住宅の建物に変わっていっています。

　ですから幽霊となったあなたがたは、まさに

go nowhere, so you'll return to your home. After that, some of you, of course, will talk every day to your family, your husband or wife or children, and they feel something evil at that time, but they can do nothing for you because they cannot see you and they cannot reply to you. No one in this world officially can teach you in this condition.

Only religion or religious people can teach you. If your occupation in this world is quite opposite to that of religious people, you'll feel great difficulty in understanding. So, I've been recommending that even one book of mine will be a hint for you, the lay person, I mean the people who don't have enough knowledge or interest in religious matter.

〝迷える羊〟です。どこにも行けないので自宅に帰ってから、やはり家族、夫や妻、子供たちに毎日話しかけたりします。そうすると、向こうは何か嫌な感じを受けますが、あなたに何もしてくれることはできません。姿も見えなければ返事もできないからです。この状態では、あなたに教えてくれる人は、表向きの世間一般には誰もいません。

　教えることができるのは宗教、あるいは宗教を信じている人たちだけです。この世で、宗教的な人たちとは正反対の職業に就いていた人の場合は、理解するのは非常に難しく思えるでしょう。ですから、「私の書いた本の一冊だけでも、一般の方のヒントになる」とお勧めしているのです。一般の方とは、宗教的なことにあまり知識や関心がない人たちのことです。

Now, people believe in science and they think that science will resolve everything, but it is too much for science. Science can reveal only one percent of the universe. Scientists know almost nothing about our reality.

Some scientists have also a religious belief. It's OK, but scientists are usually bound to this world and the materialistic tools or machines, computers, or like that. But a computer cannot understand what is soul, what is another world, what is heaven and what is hell, so a computer is useless for the person who became a ghost already.

　今の人は「科学」を信じ、科学がすべてを解明すると思っていますが、科学を買いかぶりすぎています。科学が明らかにできるのは宇宙の１パーセントにすぎません。科学者は、私たちが明らかにしている真実に関して、ほとんど何もわかっていないのです。

　宗教的信条を持っている科学者もいますので、それなら良いのですが、科学者はたいてい、この世や唯物論的な道具、機械、コンピュータなどに縛られています。しかし、コンピュータには、魂とは何か、あの世とは何か、天国・地獄とは何かを理解することはできません。幽霊になってしまった人にはコンピュータは役に立たないのです。

4 Three Points of "Life Reflection"

1) Animal-like appetite

This reflection is a little difficult for you, especially the people who have business in another area. So, please teach that kind of people, "When you die, please remember the following: One is your life, of course, this time. Was your life greedy or not, or have you been greedy or not? I mean, didn't you have too much greed in your life? Please think about that." You cannot understand what is greed, but I want to say that, if you live honestly, you can understand if you are greedy or not.

4　生前の自分を振り返るための
　　三つのポイント

①強すぎる動物的欲求（貪^{とん}）

　この反省というのは、なかなか難しいことです。特に、他の分野で仕事をしている人には難しいので、そういう人には、こう教えてあげていただきたいのです。「死ぬときに次のことを思い出してください。一つは、自分の人生についてです。もちろん今回の人生です。あなたの人生において『貪^{とん}』の心はなかったか。すなわち、人生において『過ぎた欲がなかったか』どうかです。この点を考えてみてください」。「貪」とは何かはわからないものですが、正直に生きれば、自分は欲が深いかどうかはわかるものです。

Or, please think, "Is there animal appetite after your death?" Do you have animal-like appetite or animal-like want, greed? If you think so, it's miserable as a human. To be human means to live thinking that, "I am a soul" and "I was made by God in the ancient age" and "This world is just a school for me to train my soul." This is the orthodoxical thinking of a religious person.

If you have lived animal-like, and after your death, if you feel animal appetite, it's very sad. I mean, in this context, animal appetite includes the sex-oriented attitude, and of course, the food-oriented attitude or money or some valuable things-oriented attitude, or just fear of something which is poisonous for you, or

　あるいは、「自分には、死んでからも動物的な欲求があるか」を考えてみてください。動物的欲求や動物的欲望、貪欲さがあるかどうかです。あると思えたら、それは人間として、あわれなことです。人間であるとは、「自分とは魂であり、はるかなる昔に神によって創られた存在である。この世は魂修行のための学校にすぎない」と考えて生きることです。これが宗教的人間としての正統的な考え方です。

　動物のような生き方をしてきて、死後も動物的欲求を感じるとしたら、非常に悲しいことです。この場合の動物的欲求とは、性欲中心の生き方や食欲中心の生き方、また、金銭や高価なものばかりを追い求める生き方です。あるいは、自分を害するものに対する恐怖や、自分が得することばかりを好む生き方です。そういう人生は、霊的には

just to like the things which are good for you only. No spiritual value in that life. It's animal appetite. If you lose your body, you can do no animal–like activities. They are useless. So, you must be an existence beyond animal.

2) Anger

And, please reflect on your anger in your life. Your anger is really effective to the people who are following you, for example, if you are a teacher, sometimes you scold your students. Formally, sometimes, it's good. But in the common sense, if you want to get angry, it just means that you've lost your peace of mind and made some kind of difficulties in this world

価値がありません。それが動物的欲求です。肉体がなくなると動物的な活動は何ひとつできなくなり、役に立たなくなります。したがって、動物を超えた存在でなければなりません。

②怒りの心（瞋<ruby>じん</ruby>）

　また、自分が生きていたときの「瞋<ruby>じん</ruby>」（怒り）についても反省してみてください。立場が下の人たちに対して怒ることは、確かに効果があります。たとえば、先生は生徒を叱ることがあります。表向きにはそれが正しい場合もありますが、通常の場合は、怒りが込み上げてくると心の平静が失われて、世間に迷惑をかけるだけです。ですから自分の怒りについて、深く振り返ってみるこ

only. So, please see deep into your anger, and if you did too much, please reflect on that and want to change your anger into blessing others.

3) Materialistic thinking

And, the most difficult thing is, if you have a tendency of monopolism, I mean, the materialistic thinking only, you can find no materialistic-like thing in another world. You can see, of course, something. Ah, yeah. People are living in another world, and there can be seen a lot of buildings or houses. But in the true meaning, they are nothing. You can go through the houses and you can go through the bodies of other people because they also are

とです。行きすぎていた場合は反省し、その「怒り」を人に対する「祝福」に変えようと思ってみてください。

③唯物論的な考え方

　そして、最も難しいのは、モノポリズムの傾向性、すなわち唯物論的な考え方で固まっている人は、あの世では唯物論的なものには出合えないということです。もちろん、目に見えるものがあることはあります。そうなのです。あの世にも人々は生きており、ビルや家もたくさん見ることができますが、それらは実際には「無」なのです。家も、人の体も、通り抜けることができます。それらも「幽霊」だからです。どんなものも通り抜けてしまい、何ひとつつかむことはできません。そ

ghosts. So, you can go through everything and you cannot grasp anything. At this time, you must recognize that this is the first experience, but the world is not materialistic.

Then, if you have received experience or influence from Karl Marx-like thinking, please abandon that kind of thinking and please believe in God and God's teaching. Even if you have been laughing at them, it's your mistake. So, please say, "I'm very sorry to you. I misunderstood you. I, myself, was bad, evil to you." This is very important.

But common people cannot change their attitude of mind, so I repeatedly have been teaching you that, "This world is not realistic, this is just a training room for you. Believe

のとき、「こんな経験は初めてだ」と認識するに違いありませんが、世界は唯物的なものではないのです。

　したがって、カール・マルクス的な思想を学んだ経験があったり、その影響を受けたことがある方は、そういった思想は捨てて、神を信じ、神の教えを信じてください。信じる人たちを嘲笑(あざわら)ってきたとしても、それはあなたの間違いですので、「本当に申し訳ありません。私の誤解でした。私が悪かったのです」と謝ってください。それが非常に大切です。

　しかし、普通の人は心の態度を変えることができませんので、私は繰り返し、こうお伝えしています。「この世は実在の世界ではなく、トレーニングルームにすぎません。神仏を信じてくださ

in God or Buddha. Another world is the real world, and you don't have any flesh-like bodies, indeed. So, don't have attachment to your bodies. You can be supplied, of course, by some supplement or food to survive in this world, but it's not everything. You can earn money, of course, but you cannot bring it to heaven or hell, either."

So, please think about if you are materialistic or not. Be spiritual. People who appear on TV usually laugh at such kind of people who believe in ghosts or who believe in God or believers of some kind of sect or so. Their appearances are quite different, but only one truth is in it.

い。あの世が実在の世界であり、本来、肉体は
ないので、肉体に執着してはいけません。もち
ろん、この世で生きていくために栄養や食物をと
ることはできますが、それがすべてではありませ
ん。お金を稼ぐこともできますが、お金も天国や
地獄に持って還ることはできません」。

　どうか、自分は唯物論的になっていないかどう
か、考えてみてください。霊的であってくださ
い。テレビに出ている人たちは、幽霊を信じる人
や神を信じる人、何らかの宗教宗派の信者を笑い
者にするのが普通です。ただ、そういう人たちの
外見はさまざまであっても、その中を唯一の真理
が貫いています。

This world is not the real one.

This is a false one or a disguised world,

So you are just experiencing this world.

And, of course,

You came from another world

And are reborn to this world,

And again depart this world

For another world.

And, where you should go is determined

By your deeds only.

What you did in this world

Will determine where you should go.

So, I've been saying that,

"Every day, do good things.

Every day, think that

この世は真実の世界ではないのです。

この世は仮の世であり、見せかけの世界であり

人はこの世で経験を積んでいるにすぎません。

やはり人間は

あの世から来て

この世に生まれ変わり

再びこの世からあの世へと

旅立っていくのです。

そして、人がどこに行くべきかは

「行い」のみによって決まります。

あなたがこの世でなしたことが

あなたの行き先を決めるのです。

ですから、私はいつもこう説いてきました。

「毎日、『善』を行ってください。

毎日、『今日が最後だ。

This is the last time for you.

This is the only day for you.

Please live happily in the real meaning,

And say good things to others.

Or, like Santa Claus, you should be kind

To your children or other children."

These kinds of things are your reflection.

Improvement: "progress" of the Fourfold Path

And, improvement. "Is there any improvement in this world? While you have lived in this world, what did you do to this world? Was it a good thing that you lived in this world or not? Was this a bad thing for everyone or for God?"

今日一日しかない』と思ってください。

本当の意味において幸福に生き

人に対して良き言葉を発し

サンタクロースのように、自分の子供や

他の子供たちに優しくしてあげてください」。

こういったことが

あなたが「反省」すべきことです。

向上――四正道の「発展」

　そして、「向上」です。「この世において、何
らかの向上はあるか。あなたはこの世に生きてい
たとき、世の中に対して何をしたか。あなたがこ
の世に生きていたのは良いことだったのか。人々
や神にとって良くないことだったのか」。それ

It's the value of your life. Please think about that.

What have you done in your life? Can you count that? For example, your business or your family or what you thought about and your influence on other people. I said these Fourfold Truths.

が、あなたの人生の価値です。どうか、そのこと
を考えてみてください。

　自分は人生で何をしたかを数え上げることがで
きるでしょうか。たとえば仕事や家族について。
あるいは、他の人たちについて何を考え、どのよ
うな影響を与えたでしょうか。私は、こうした四
つの真理を説きました。

5 Spread This Truth to Have
All People Live Priceless Lives

After that, please believe in your guardian spirit and guiding spirit. Call them and ask them, "What should I do from now on?" They will say something, "Oh, you are destined to go to hell," or "Some kind of animal hell," or "Villain hell," or "Devil-like hell, black and evil and fearful hell," or "You can be a spiritual being and go to the next level, I mean the fifth dimension or more than that." Or, sometimes you will find that yourself is an angel. It's quite different.

5　価値ある人生を生きるための
　　真理をすべての人に

　そこから後は、守護・指導霊を信じてください。
彼らを呼んで「これからどうすればいいでしょう
か」と聞いてみれば、何か言ってくれるでしょ
う。「ああ、あなたは地獄行きで決まりです」と
か、「畜生道みたいなところです」とか、「無頼
漢地獄です」あるいは「悪魔がいるような地獄で
す。暗黒で凶悪で恐ろしい地獄です」。あるいは、
「霊存在となって次の段階、すなわち五次元か、
それ以上の次元に行けるでしょう」。あるいは、
天使になっている自分に気づくこともあります。
そこには大きな差があります。

But I just want to say,

"All you have learned in this life,

Especially learned by religion,

Happy Science books, will do

A good thing for you in your next lives."

This is the starting point of *dendo*.

So, please think that you are very priceless,

I mean you have a value in your life.

Please think

It's a great chance for you to live.

All I want to say is that,

"You are not destined to die tomorrow."

You have another day or another year to live.

You have enough time

To change your course of lives.

ただ、言っておきたいのは
「今世で学んだことはすべて、
特に幸福の科学の本を通して学んだことは
来世であなたの役に立つ」ということです。
ここが伝道の出発点です。
どうか自分自身を
このうえなく価値ある存在だと思ってください。
あなたの人生は価値ある人生なのです。
「生きる」ということは、自分にとって
大きなチャンスであると思ってください。

これだけは言っておきたいと思うのは
「あなたは明日死ぬと
決まっているわけではない」ということです。
次の一日、次の一年を生きることができ、
人生の行路を変える時間は十分にあります。

So, please think and believe my words

And spread this Truth to your neighbors

And to your country

And to the people of the world.

This is "The Ghost Condition."

Could you understand what I said? OK? If there is any question, please ask me.

ですから、どうか、私の言葉について考え、

私の言葉を信じて、この真理を

身近な人や自分の国の人たち、

世界中の人たちに伝えてください。

以上が「幽霊の条件」です。

わかりましたか。よろしいですか。何か質問が

あれば、どうぞ。

Q How Can We Tell What Type of Spirit is Influencing Us?

Question Happy Science conducts various spiritual readings on paranormal phenomena, but most people don't understand what is influencing them. Is there a way to tell the difference between a ghost or space people or *ikiryo*—living spirit or animal spirit? How can we tell what is influencing us?

It's difficult to tell a ghost from *ikiryo*

Ryuho Okawa It's difficult. If they are just outsiders or not, if they are our followers or they want to be our teachers or lecturers, it's

214

質問　自分に影響を与えている
　　　霊の種類を見分けるには

質問　幸福の科学では、超常現象に関するさまざまなリーディングが行われていますが、ほとんどの人は、何が自分に影響を与えているのかわかりません。幽霊なのか、宇宙人なのか、生霊なのか、動物霊なのか、違いを見分ける方法はありますでしょうか。何が自分に影響を与えているのかを見分けるには、どうすればよいのでしょうか。

「幽霊」と「生霊」を見分けることの難しさ

大川隆法　それは難しいことです。その人が外部の人なのかどうか。信者や当会の講師になろうとしている人なら、それがわかるようになるのは

a professional way to understand that, but if they are lay people, to tell the differences of the ghosts is very difficult for them. So, at that time, please teach them that, "This is an important teaching from a heavenly existence," or "This is a bad example of the ghost phenomenon." Just make some kind of explanation only.

They cannot understand clearly about that. For example, to tell a real ghost from *ikiryo* is very difficult, even for me. Sometimes, I misunderstood it's a ghost, but it was an *ikiryo* that came from a living person. So, it's very difficult.

It's almost the same. I mean a ghost is an existence of energy. It's a thinking energy. Thinking energy is a ghost, itself, but in this context, a ghost is accompanied by posthumous

「プロへの道」ですが、在家《ざいけ》の方であれば、幽霊の違いを見分けるのは、きわめて難しいことです。そういう時は、「これが天上界の存在からの大切な教えです。こちらは、悪いほうの幽霊現象の例です」と説明だけしてあげてください。

　その点は明確にはわからないものです。たとえば私であっても、本物の幽霊と生霊を見分けるのは非常に難しいことです。幽霊だと思っていたら実は違って、生きている人の生霊だったこともあります。実に難しいのです。

　それらはほとんど同じものなのです。要するに、幽霊とはエネルギーとしての存在なのです。「思考するエネルギー体」です。思考するエネルギー体が幽霊そのものなのですが、ここで言う幽

or astral body of humankind. It's a surface of the soul, so it looks like as he or she lives.

But the real existence is not such kind of figure. It's like the light, itself. They are just shedding their light. It's some kind of plasma–like existence. So, even if the real person in this world sheds that kind of thinking energy, for example, to me, I sometimes misunderstand that, "Is it a ghost or the thinking of a real person?" and hearing them carefully, I will understand.

Their teachings tell who they are

Sometimes, *ikiryo* is the real thinking of the real

霊は、人間としての幽体をまとっています。幽体とは魂のいちばん外側の部分であり、その人が生きていた時そのままの姿に見えるのです。

しかし、実在としての存在はそういった姿はとっておらず、光そのもののような存在です。ただただ光を放っているだけなので、ある種のプラズマのような存在です。ですから、この世に実際に生きている人も、たとえば私に向けて、そういう思考エネルギーを発することができるので、それが幽霊なのか生きている人の考えなのか、私でも間違うことがありますが、相手の話を注意深く聞いていくと、わかるのです。

何者かを見分ける基準は「教えの中身」

「現実に生きている人の念い」と「守護霊」が

person and his or her guardian spirit combined. If it is a higher spirit or not, it depends on the teachings only. Only the teachings can tell who they are. I mean, if you read some kind of spiritual saying or interview, and if you feel something good or something bad from them, it concludes who they are.

But when it comes to the Satan-like existences, common people cannot understand because they have very much experience and knowledge regarding how to control human beings.

For example, recently, we've found that Mao Tse-tung, the founder of the Communist Party of China, is the largest devil of this Earth, and the Soviet Union founder or the leader of the Russian Revolution, I mean Lenin, and his

合体して生霊になっている場合もあります。それが高級霊かどうかを見分けるには、「教えの中身」しかありません。それが何者であるかを示すものは、「教え」だけです。すなわち、ある霊言を読んで感じられるのが、良いものか、それとも悪いものか。その霊の正体についての結論は、そこにあります。

　ただ、それがサタンのような存在である場合は、普通の人にはわかりません。彼らは、人の心を操る方法に関して経験も知識も非常に豊富だからです。

　たとえば最近、中国共産党の創立者、毛沢東が地球最大の悪魔であることがわかりました。また、ソ連の創立者でロシア革命の指導者であるレーニンや、その後継者のスターリンも悪魔です。大変な驚きです。おまけに、彼らの敵であったア

successor Stalin are also devils. Oh, astonishing. And, in addition to that, their enemy, Adolf Hitler is also a devil. Oh! Incredible! Devil vs. devil was the real meaning of the Second World War. It's difficult. People are apt to think that one side is good and another side is evil, but sometimes evil vs. evil can happen in this world.

So, you must be careful about that. Even the famous people might not be angels, and someone who was seen as a small person could really be a great person. It really happens. And sometimes, the people who were murdered in this world, assassinated I mean, like Lincoln or Kennedy or Ryoma Sakamoto, or people like Shoin Yoshida or Hanpeita Takechi, are

ドルフ・ヒットラーも悪魔だというのですから、信じ難いことです！　「悪魔 対 悪魔」というのが第二次世界大戦の真相だったわけです。難しいものです。「一方が善で、もう一方は悪である」と思われがちですが、この世では、時には「悪 対 悪」ということも起こりうるのです。

　ですから、この点は注意しなければいけません。有名な人でも天使ではないかもしれないし、小さく見られていた人が偉大な人物であることもあります。そうしたことが実際にあるのです。リンカンやケネディ、坂本龍馬など、この世で暗殺された人や、吉田松陰や武市半平太のような人は、この世だけで見れば悲惨な人生ではありますが、この世の中に神や天使の足跡を遺し

miserable in this world only, but they left footprints of God or angels in this world.

Every day, every time is a teaching

So, it's very difficult to understand what kind of spirit it is. There need long time to judge. But you, yourself, can understand what you are in the near future, not so long future. So, if you are not a self-concentrated person and not a self-preservation-oriented person, you can understand what the spirit said is evil or good in the honest mind.

If you have greed or you are greedy, you cannot understand, and if you have too much confidence in you, and it's beyond what you can

たわけです。

毎日、あらゆる機会が「教え」である

　というわけで、どんな種類の霊なのかを理解することは、きわめて難しいことです。それが判定できるようになるには長い時間が必要です。ただ、自分自身が何者であるかは、いずれ、そう遠くない未来においてわかるでしょう。自己中心的だったり自己保存的傾向が強かったりする人でなければ、自分の正直な心に照らして、霊の言っていることが悪か善か、わかります。

　貪の心がある人には、わかりません。自分に自信がありすぎて、抑えが利かなくなっている場合は、「天狗」的な存在になってしまうでしょう。

keep, you will be a *tengu*, a long-nose goblin-like existence. At that time, you cannot hear correctly the words from heaven or words from hell. So, be honest and obey God's teachings, and rely on your colleagues of the religious group.

There are a lot of mistakes which will be waiting you. But every day, every time is a teaching. You can find out what the truth is and what the spirit is and what kind of spirit it is. It's just the way to the professional leader of the religion.

So, there is no complete answer for you. Each effort will lead you to a greater position, and you can be a spiritual teacher. I think so.

そうなると、「天国からの言葉」と「地獄からの言葉」を正しく聞き分けることはできません。ですから正直を旨として、神の教えに素直に従い、教団の仲間を信頼してください。

　間違いを犯すことも数多く出てくるでしょう。しかし、毎日が「教え」であり、あらゆる機会が「教え」であるのです。「真理とは何か」「霊とは何か」「それがどのような霊か」、わかるようになっていきます。それこそが、プロの宗教指導者への道にほかなりません。

　ご質問に対する完璧な答えはありませんが、一つひとつ精進を積み重ねることで、自らの境地を高め、霊的指導者になっていくことができると思います。

Afterword

In simple words, your life is not limited to this world only. You have past life, present life, and future life.

Make efforts every day to return successfully to God or Buddha. Do not complain too much about worldly unhappiness regarding materials.

The kind of world that you see in your dreams is actually the real world.

When you are suffering a lot spiritually, just pray. First abandon worldly desires, and try to live a life of gratitude and giving back.

Jan. 28, 2020

Master & CEO of Happy Science Group

Ryuho Okawa

あとがき

　簡単に言えば、あなたの人生はこの世限りでは
ない。過去世があって、現世があって、未来世が
ある。

　無事、神仏の元に還れるよう、日々努力するこ
とだ。この世の物質的な不幸を嘆き過ぎるな。

　あなたが夢の中で見るような世界が、本当の世
界なのだ。

　とても霊的に苦しい時は、ただ祈るがよい。こ
の世的欲望をいったん捨て去って、感謝と報恩に
生きようとすることだ。

2020 年 1 月 28 日

幸福の科学グループ創始者兼総裁

大川隆法

『ザ・ポゼッション』大川隆法著作関連書籍

『神秘の法』
『真のエクソシスト』
『悪魔からの防衛術』
『エクソシスト概論』
　　　　　　（いずれも幸福の科学出版刊）

ザ・ポゼッション
——憑依の真相——

2020 年 2 月 7 日　初版第 1 刷
2020 年 3 月 10 日　　　第 2 刷

著　者　　大　川　隆　法

発行所　　幸福の科学出版株式会社

〒107-0052 東京都港区赤坂 2 丁目 10 番 8 号
TEL(03) 5573-7700
https://www.irhpress.co.jp/

印刷・製本　株式会社 研文社

真のエクソシスト

身体が重い、抑うつ、悪夢、金縛り、幻聴——。それは悪霊による「憑依」かもしれない。フィクションを超えた最先端のエクソシスト論、ついに公開。

1,600円

悪魔からの防衛術
「リアル・エクソシズム」入門

現代の「心理学」や「法律学」の奥にある、霊的な「正義」と「悪」の諸相が明らかに。"目に見えない脅威"から、あなたの人生を護る降魔入門。

1,600円

生霊論
運命向上の智慧と秘術

それは、あなたの毎日に影響を与えている、目に見えない力——。生霊にまつわるあらゆる事象をズバッと解説。「生霊に影響されない」「自分が生霊にならない」対策とは。

1,600円

幸福の科学出版

あなたの知らない地獄の話。

天国に還るために今からできること

無頼漢、土中、擂鉢、畜生、焦熱、阿修羅、色情、餓鬼、悪魔界──、現代社会に合わせて変化している地獄の最新事情とその脱出法を解説した必読の一書。

1,500円

あなたは死んだらどうなるか？

あの世への旅立ちとほんとうの終活

「老い」「病気」「死後の旅立ち」──。地獄に行かないために、生前から実践すべき「天国に還るための方法」とは。知っておきたいあの世の真実。

1,500円

新しい霊界入門

人は死んだらどんな体験をする?

あの世の生活って、どんなもの? すべての人に知ってほしい、最先端の霊界情報が満載の一書。渡部昇一氏の恩師・佐藤順太氏の霊言を同時収録。

1,500円

※表示価格は本体価格（税別）です。

アメリカには見えない
イランの本心

ハメネイ師守護霊・
ソレイマニ司令官の霊言

イランは独裁国家か、それとも民主主義国家か。アメリカによる攻撃に正義はあったのか。マスコミ報道では知ることのできないイラン司令官殺害の"真相"に迫る。

1,400円

イエス　ヤイドロン
トス神の霊言

神々の考える現代的正義

香港デモに正義はあるのか。LGBTの問題点とは。地球温暖化は人類の危機なのか。中東問題の解決に向けて。神々の語る「正義」と「未来」が人類に示される。

1,400円

イギリス・イランの
転換点について

ジョンソン首相・ロウハニ大統領・
ハメネイ師・トランプ大統領守護霊の霊言

ＥＵ離脱でイギリスは復活するのか？ 米とイランの和解はあるのか？ 各国の首脳に本心を訊く！ 安倍首相・グレタ氏守護霊、ガイアの霊言を同時収録。

1,400円

幸福の科学出版

人類史を変える「歴史的瞬間」が誕生した。
1991年7月15日、東京ドーム。
——これは、映画を超えた真実。

夜明けを信じて。

2020年秋 ROADSHOW

製作総指揮・原作 大川隆法

田中宏明　千眼美子　長谷川奈央　芦川よしみ　石橋保

監督/赤羽博　音楽/水澤有一　脚本/大川咲也加　製作/幸福の科学出版　製作協力/ARI Production　ニュースター・プロダクション
制作プロダクション/ジャンゴフィルム　配給/日活　配給協力/東京テアトル　©2020 IRH Press

幸福の科学グループのご案内

宗教、教育、政治、出版などの活動を通じて、地球的ユートピアの実現を目指しています。

幸福の科学

1986年に立宗。信仰の対象は、地球系霊団の最高大霊、主エル・カンターレ。世界100カ国以上の国々に信者を持ち、全人類救済という尊い使命のもと、信者は、「愛」と「悟り」と「ユートピア建設」の教えの実践、伝道に励んでいます。

（2020年1月現在）

愛　幸福の科学の「愛」とは、与える愛です。これは、仏教の慈悲や布施の精神と同じことです。信者は、仏法真理をお伝えすることを通して、多くの方に幸福な人生を送っていただくための活動に励んでいます。

悟り　「悟り」とは、自らが仏の子であることを知るということです。教学や精神統一によって心を磨き、智慧を得て悩みを解決すると共に、天使・菩薩の境地を目指し、より多くの人を救える力を身につけていきます。

ユートピア建設　私たち人間は、地上に理想世界を建設するという尊い使命を持って生まれてきています。社会の悪を押しとどめ、善を推し進めるために、信者はさまざまな活動に積極的に参加しています。

海外支援・災害支援

国内外の世界で貧困や災害、心の病で苦しんでいる人々に対しては、現地メンバーや支援団体と連携して、物心両面にわたり、あらゆる手段で手を差し伸べています。

自殺を減らそうキャンペーン

年間約2万人の自殺者を減らすため、全国各地で街頭キャンペーンを展開しています。

 公式サイト **www.withyou-hs.net**

ヘレンの会

ヘレン・ケラーを理想として活動する、ハンディキャップを持つ方とボランティアの会です。視聴覚障害者、肢体不自由な方々に仏法真理を学んでいただくための、さまざまなサポートをしています。

 公式サイト **www.helen-hs.net**

入会のご案内

幸福の科学では、大川隆法総裁が説く仏法真理（ぶっぽうしんり）をもとに、「どうすれば幸福になれるのか、また、他の人を幸福にできるのか」を学び、実践しています。

（入会）

仏法真理を学んでみたい方へ

大川隆法総裁の教えを信じ、学ぼうとする方なら、どなたでも入会できます。入会された方には、『入会版「正心法語」（しょうしんほうご）』が授与されます。

ネット入会　入会ご希望の方はネットからも入会できます。
happy-science.jp/joinus

（三帰（さんき）誓願（せいがん））

信仰をさらに深めたい方へ

仏弟子としてさらに信仰を深めたい方は、仏・法・僧（ぶっぽうそう）の三宝（さんぼう）への帰依を誓う「三帰誓願式」を受けることができます。三帰誓願者には、『仏説・正心法語』『祈願文①（きがんもん）』『祈願文②』『エル・カンターレへの祈り』が授与されます。

幸福の科学 サービスセンター
TEL 03-5793-1727
受付時間/
火〜金：10〜20時
土・日祝：10〜18時
（月曜を除く）

幸福の科学 公式サイト
happy-science.jp

仏法真理塾「サクセスNo.1」

全国に本校・拠点・支部校を展開する、幸福の科学による信仰教育の機関です。小学生・中学生・高校生を対象に、信仰教育・徳育にウエイトを置きつつ、将来、社会人として活躍するための学力養成にも力を注いでいます。

TEL 03-5750-0751（東京本校）

エンゼルプランV　TEL 03-5750-0757

幼少時からの心の教育を大切にして、信仰をベースにした幼児教育を行っています。

不登校児支援スクール「ネバー・マインド」　TEL 03-5750-1741

心の面からのアプローチを重視して、不登校の子供たちを支援しています。

ユー・アー・エンゼル！（あなたは天使！）運動

一般社団法人 ユー・アー・エンゼル　TEL 03-6426-7797

障害児の不安や悩みに取り組み、ご両親を励まし、勇気づける、
障害児支援のボランティア運動を展開しています。

NPO活動支援

学校からのいじめ追放を目指し、さまざまな社会提言をしています。また、各地でのシンポジウムや学校への啓発ポスター掲示等に取り組む一般財団法人「いじめから子供を守ろうネットワーク」を支援しています。

公式サイト mamoro.org　ブログ blog.mamoro.org
相談窓口 TEL.03-5544-8989

百歳まで生きる会

「百歳まで生きる会」は、生涯現役人生を掲げ、友達づくり、生きがいづくりをめざしている幸福の科学のシニア信者の集まりです。

シニア・プラン21

生涯反省で人生を再生・新生し、希望に満ちた生涯現役人生を生きる仏法真理道場です。定期的に開催される研修には、年齢を問わず、多くの方が参加しています。全世界212カ所（国内197カ所、海外15カ所）で開校中。

【東京校】TEL 03-6384-0778　FAX 03-6384-0779
メール senior-plan@kofuku-no-kagaku.or.jp

幸福実現党 釈量子サイト
shaku-ryoko.net

Twitter
釈量子@shakuryoko
で検索

党の機関紙
「幸福実現NEWS」

政治

幸福実現党

ないゆうがいかん
内憂外患の国難に立ち向かうべく、2009年5月に幸福実現党を立党しました。創立者である大川隆法党総裁の精神的指導のもと、宗教だけでは解決できない問題に取り組み、幸福を具体化するための力になっています。

幸福実現党　党員募集中

あなたも幸福を実現する政治に参画しませんか。

- ○ 幸福実現党の理念と綱領、政策に賛同する18歳以上の方なら、どなたでも参加いただけます。
- ○ 党費：正党員（年額5千円［学生 年額2千円］）、特別党員（年額10万円以上）、家族党員（年額2千円）
- ○ 党員資格は党費を入金された日から1年間です。
- ○ 正党員、特別党員の皆様には機関紙「幸福実現NEWS（党員版）」（不定期発行）が送付されます。

＊申込書は、下記、幸福実現党公式サイトでダウンロードできます。
住所：〒107-0052　東京都港区赤坂2-10-8 6階 幸福実現党本部

TEL 03-6441-0754　**FAX** 03-6441-0764
公式サイト hr-party.jp

幸福の科学グループ事業

幸福の科学出版

出版メディア事業

大川隆法総裁の仏法真理の書を中心に、ビジネス、自己啓発、小説など、さまざまなジャンルの書籍・雑誌を出版しています。他にも、映画事業、文学・学術発展のための振興事業、テレビ・ラジオ番組の提供など、幸福の科学文化を広げる事業を行っています。

アー・ユー・ハッピー？
are-you-happy.com

ザ・リバティ
the-liberty.com

ザ・ファクト
マスコミが報道しない「事実」を世界に伝えるネット・オピニオン番組

YouTubeにて随時好評配信中！

幸福の科学出版
TEL 03-5573-7700
公式サイト irhpress.co.jp

ザ・ファクト 検索

ニュースター・プロダクション

芸能文化事業

「新時代の美」を創造する芸能プロダクションです。多くの方々に良き感化を与えられるような魅力あふれるタレントを世に送り出すべく、日々、活動しています。

公式サイト newstarpro.co.jp

ARI Production

タレント一人ひとりの個性や魅力を引き出し、「新時代を創造するエンターテインメント」をコンセプトに、世の中に精神的価値のある作品を提供していく芸能プロダクションです。

公式サイト aripro.co.jp

大川隆法　講演会のご案内

大川隆法総裁の講演会が全国各地で開催されています。講演のなかでは、毎回、「世界教師」としての立場から、幸福な人生を生きるための心の教えをはじめ、世界各地で起きている宗教対立、紛争、国際政治や経済といった時事問題に対する指針など、日本と世界がさらなる繁栄の未来を実現するための道筋が示されています。

2019年12月17日 さいたまスーパーアリーナ「新しき繁栄の時代

2019年10月6日 ザ ウェスティン ハーバー
キャッスル トロント(カナダ)
「The Reason We Are Here」

2019年7月5日 福岡国際センター
「人生に自信を持て」

2019年3月3日 グランド ハイアット 台北(台湾)
「愛は憎しみを超えて」

2019年7月13日 ホテル イースト21東京
「幸福への論点」

講演会には、どなたでもご参加いただけます。
最新の講演会の開催情報はこちらへ。　➡

大川隆法総裁公式サイト
https://ryuho-okawa.org